Lessons from the New Testament

By Dorothy Tatum

Published in the United States of America by:
Cobb Publishing
704 E. Main St
Charleston, AR 72933
(479) 747-8372
CobbPublishing@gmail.com
www.CobbPublishing.com

ISBN: 978-1-960858-71-9

Dear Student:

We are beginning an exciting new year of study in the New Testament. In order for you to get the most possible out of our lessons, you should keep your notebook handy and prepare your lessons each week before class time. It will be more fun **if** we are all prepared. Each week you can earn points by having your lesson done and knowing your memory verse.

We want our class to be fun, but, most of all we are here to learn more about the Bible and to please God .We can do that and have fun too! We hope you will enjoy this class.

Anytime you need to talk to me or have a question about your lesson, please call at the number listed below. If I don't answer, leave a message and I will call you back.

I'm so glad to have you in this class.

Teacher's Name _____

Phone Number _____

The Bible

Did you know
that when you carry the Bible,
Satan has a headache,
when you open it, he collapses,
when he sees you reading it,
he loses his strength,
AND
when you stand on the Word of God,
Satan can't hurt you!

NEW TESTAMENT

FOUR GOSPELS:
Matthew

Mark

Luke

John

ACTS OF THE APOSTLES
Acts

21 LETTERS (EPISTLES) TO PEOPLE, CHURCHES AND AREAS:

Romans	1 Thessalonians	James
1 Corinthians	2 Thessalonians	1 Peter
2 Corinthians	1 Timothy	2 Peter
Galatians	2 Timothy	1 John
Ephesians	Titus	2 John
Philippians	Philemon	3 John
Colossians	Hebrews	Jude

PROPHECY
Revelation

BIBLE FACTS I SHOULD KNOW:

1. Three ages: Patriarchal — Mosaic — Christian

2. 27 books in the New Testament: 39 books in the Old Testament; 66 books Total.

3. 1189 Chapters in the Bible.

4. It took about 1600 years to whit- Bible.

5. 8 men wrote the New Testament.

6. 40 men wrote the Bible.

7. Psalms 117 is shortest chapter in the Bible. Psalms 119 is the longest chapter in the Bible.

8. Bible written in these languages: Hebrew, Aramaic, Greek.

9. Purpose of the Bible: To tell man of Jesus saving power.

10. Theme of Bible: Redemption of man.

11. Moses wrote Genesis.

12. John wrote Revelations.

13. Book of Acts: History of Church.

14. Inspiration of Bible: God breathed.

15. Moses wrote first 5 books of Bible—called the Pentateuch (Law)

16. Joint wrote 5 books—John, 1, 2, 3 John, and Revelation.

17. Shortest verse in the Bible is John 11:35.

18. The second coming of Christ is mentioned in every book of the New Testament' except Philemon

19. God's name does not appear in the Book of Esther.

20. The only woman whose age appears in the Bible is Sarah, Abraham's wife.

BIBLE FACTS I SHOULD LEARN

TESTAMENT means COVENANT or AGREEMENT.

GOD made a COVENANT at Mt. Sinai with the Jewish people. (Law of Moses)

OLD TESTAMENT—39 Books, 32 Writers

The Old Testament gives History of man from creation to 400 years before Christ.

There are FIVE divisions in the Old Testament:

Law (Pentateuch), History, Poetry, Major Prophets, Minor Prophets.

NEW TESTAMENT—27 Books, 8 Writers:

Matthew, Mark, Luke, John, Paul, Peter James, Jude.

The New Testament Is Gods covenant with man who serve Him through Christ. There are FOUR divisions in the New Testament:

- <u>Biography</u> (Christ's birth, life, death, resurrection),
- <u>History</u> of early church (Church established, Acts 2, early growth of church.),
- <u>Letters</u> to People and Churches (Instruction for living Christian life.),
- <u>Prophecy</u>.

GOSPEL—Good news of JESUS CHRIST

TO UNDERSTAND THE BIBLE, WE SHOULD KNOW THAT IT INCLUDES 3 AGES.

Patriarchal Age		Mosaic Age		Christian Age
2500 year period	**R**	1500 year period	**T**	Day of Pentecost, 'til...
	E		**H**	
God gave instructions to heads of families.	**D**	Also called the Jewish age.	**E**	God's laws for us through Christ
		Laws given to Moses at Mt. Sinai		
Some important people of this time:	**S**	Some important people of this time:	**C**	Some important people of this time:
	E		**R**	
Adam	**A**	Moses	**O**	Christ
Noah		Joshua		Matthew
Abraham		Saul	**S**	Peter
Isaac		David		Paul
Jacob		Solomon	**S**	Timothy
Joseph		Daniel		Barnabas
		Isaiah		
		Jeremiah*		

*Prophesied that God would make a New Covenant.

THE

Gospels

BIRTH OF JESUS

MEMORY VERSE: Luke 2:19

The first four books of the New Testament, Matthew, Mark, Luke and John are called the Gospels. In each book a part of the story of Jesus birth, life, and death are told. Even though the author told in his words a part of the story, it all fits together perfectly.

The author of each of these 4 gospels is shown at the beginning of the book. Look at each one and write the author's name beside the book.

Matthew _____

Mark _____

Luke _____

John _____

Matthew 1:1 tells us of two prominent Bible characters from whom Jesus descended. They were _____ and _____.

ABOUT JOHN

LUKE, Chapter 1

1. Vs. 17 tells us that John had a special purpose. He was to help prepare people for the coming of the _____.

2. Vs. 5-7. There was a priest named _____ and his wife _____ who had no _____.

3. Vs. 13 tells us that an _____ spoke to Zacharias and told him he and Elizabeth would have a _____ named _____.

4. Vs. 20. Because Zacharias doubted, what happened to him?

    _____

5. Vs. 57 tells us Elizabeth gave birth to a _____. As they were deciding what to call the baby, Zacharias _____ (vs. 63) his name is _____.

6. After not being able to speak for months, vs. 64 tells us that Zacharias

_____ and _____ God.

LUKE, Chapter 7
7. Vs. 20 tells us a longer name for John. What was it? _____

REMEMBER — John's special purpose was to help prepare for Christ's coming to earth to teach and save people. Jesus was the Messiah the Jewish people had looked for so long.

JESUS' BIRTH

MATTHEW, Chapter 1
1. Vs. 18 tells us Jesus mother was to be _____. She was to

have a baby but had no husband, even though she was engaged to Joseph.

Her child would come as a miracle from God by the _____

_____.

LUKE 2:1-20. Read these verses.
2. Vs. 4 and 5 tell us Joseph and Mary were in _____ because

they were required to be there to be counted and _____.

3. Vs. 8-14 tell us about some people who were interested in Jesus' birth. Read these verses carefully and we will discuss them in class.

MATTHEW, Chapter 2
4. Vs. 1 and 2 tell of others who wanted to find this special baby. They were

the _____

5. Vs. 9 tells how the wise men found Jesus by following the

_____

6. Vs. 11 tells 3 things the wise men did when they came to where Jesus

was.

a. _____

b. _____

c. _____

BUT, all is not well here ... there is evil lurking...

7. Joseph had a _____ to escape to _____ because _____ was trying to find Jesus to _____ him. (Vs. 13)

8. Vs. 19 and 20 tell us Joseph and Mary were now free to go home to Israel because _____ was dead.

9. Vs. 23 tells us they came to live in a city called _____.

JESUS, GOD'S SON WAS BORN IN A STABLE, WRAPPED IN CLOTH, AND LAID IN A MANGER FILLED WITH STRAW. BUT, WHAT JOY HE BROUGHT TO MANKIND! IN THIS HUMBLE SURROUNDING, SHEPHERDS CAME TO VIEW HIM, ANGELS SANG GLORIOUS SONGS AND THE WISEST OF MEN FOLLOWED A STAR TO FIND HIM AND PRAISE HIM.

Our memory verse tells how his mother Mary marveled at all these things and kept them in her heart.

JESUS AS A BOY

MEMORY VERSE — Colossians 3:20

The four Gospels are _____, _____,

_____, and _____.

They tell us about Jesus: his birth, his life, his teachings and his death.

Last week we studied about Jesus special birth to a virgin named Mary. His birth was marked by a star in the sky that guided shepherds and wise men to celebrate his birth. It also caused kings to be jealous because they thought he would become a king on earth. They did not understand his kingdom was not of this world, but a spiritual kingdom.

Joseph, his earthly father, protected Jesus by taking him to Egypt for a few years until it was safe to return to their homeland.

READ MATTHEW, Chapter 2:19-23

1. How did Joseph know they could go home—who told him?

    _____ What happened to Herod? _____

    _____

2. Vs. 21 tells where they were headed _____ but vs. 22

    tells us they didn't go there but ended up in _____

    (vs. 23)

LUKE 2:40-52

1. Vs. 40 tells us Jesus grew strong in _____ and

    _____, and God's _____ was upon him.

2. Verses 41-50. Every year a special Jewish holiday was celebrated. It was

    in _____ and was called the _____ of the

    _____.

This recalled to the people the days when they were slaves in Egypt and God had delivered them when the angel passed over the land and killed the Egyptians' first born.

3. When Jesus was _____ years old he went up to Jerusalem with his parents.

4.	Joseph and Mary did not realize _____ was not with the crowd when they started home. They thought he was with _____.

5.	After a _____'s journey they began to look for Jesus, but could not find him.

6.	They decided to go back to _____ to look for him.

7.	Joseph and Mary looked for Jesus for _____ days.

8.	They found him in the_____. He was talking and listening to men who were _____.

9.	Vs. 47 tells us those who were there and heard Jesus with these men were _____ because he _____ and _____ them.

10.	Jesus' mother told him how worried they had been because he was lost. She asked why he did this. Jesus was not being disobedient, he answered her (vs. 49) "I was about my _____'s business." What did he mean? _____

_____

11.	Did Mary and Joseph understand? _____ (Vs. 50)

12.	The family went home to _____ . When the Bible says he was subject to them, what does that mean? _____

13.	Mary had known all along that Jesus was special. She didn't understand everything about this special boy, but vs. 51 tells us she kept all these special things in her _____.

14.	Vs. 52. Jesus grew in _____ and _____ and in favor with _____ and _____.

We discussed "was subject" to his parents. He was obedient. It is important for us to learn from Jesus to be obedient to our parents. If we learn obedience at home, we will be obedient at school, to the laws of the land, and most of all obedient to God! That means doing what he tells us to do in the Bible; if we are obedient we will want to be Christians and serve Him.

BAPTISM OF JESUS

MEMORY VERSE — John 1:1

Look back at Lesson 1 in your book to the section on John. Go over this section as a review.

Remember, John was to prepare the way, or go ahead of Jesus to tell the people he was coming and he was the Savior.

JOHN'S MISSION: MATTHEW 3:1-3

1. John came _____ in the wilderness of _____.

2. He told the people to _____ for the _____ was at hand.

3. "Prepare the way of the _____," John told them as the prophet _____ had said long ago.

MARK 1:1-4

1. Vs. 3 tells us in almost the same words as Matthew — "The _____ of one crying in the _____, prepare the _____ of the _____."

2. Vs. 2. Mark, the writer of this book also quoted the prophet _____.

3. John did _____ with the baptism of _____ for the _____ of sin.

4. Vs. 1 tells us this was the _____ of _____ ministry.

LUKE 3

1. Vs. 3 states the very same thing as one of the verses in Mark (see above). What chapter and verse is it? _____

2. Vs. 4 is the same as which verse in Matthew? _____ (see above)

3. In vs. 16 John makes some statements about one who is to follow him. He says he is not worthy to _____ his _____. John says Je-

sus will baptize with the _____.

WHAT KIND OF PERSON WAS JOHN THE BAPTIZER?

MATTHEW 3:4

Describe John as shown here. _____

_____

_____

MARK 1:6

Does this sound familiar? Is John described the same or differently than in Matthew? _____

How do you see John — check the spaces you think describe John.

__Rugged __Outdoorsman __Honest __Strong __Ruthless __Sharing __ City dweller __Fancy foods __Brave __Kind __Concerned __Obedient

(Clues: Luke 3:11; Luke 3:14)

JESUS' BAPTISM: READ MATTHEW 3:13-17; MARK 1:9-11; LUKE 3:21-23

1. Jesus came from at the _____ to where John was preaching and baptizing at the _____ River.

2. Did John think he was worthy to baptize Jesus? _____ Did he then baptize him? _____

3. After Jesus was baptized, the _____ opened and a _____ came and rested on Jesus.

4. A voice from Heaven said "This is my _____ in whom I am well pleased." Whose voice was this? _____

Jesus was baptized by John as an example of obedience to God. Had he sinned?_____ He did not need forgiveness of sin as we do. When we are baptized we show our obedience to God as Jesus did.

WHAT HAPPENED TO JOHN? MATTHEW 14

1. Vs. 3 tells us Herod did something to John. What did he do? _____

2. Vs. 6 and 7 tell of Herod's promise (oath) to his stepdaughter because she pleased him when she _____.

3. Vs. 8 tells us what happened to John. _____
   _____

TEMPTATIONS OF JESUS

MEMORY VERSE: Matthew 4:7

In last week's study, Jesus came to the Jordan River where John was baptizing and was himself baptized by John. God was pleased with Jesus' obedience and sent a sign—a dove and a voice from Heaven saying, "This is my beloved son."

After Jesus' baptism, God allowed some things to happen to him. We can read about them in three of the gospels; Matthew, Mark and Luke.

READ: MATTHEW 4:1-4, MARK 1:12-13, LUKE 4:1-4

1. After leaving the Jordan River area, he went into the _____.

2. What did Jesus do without? _____ For how long? _____

3. There was something/someone else present during this time. What was it?

    _____

4. During Jesus fasting time (doing without food) Satan tempted him, how?

    _____

5. Jesus said to Satan, "Man does not live by _____ alone,

    he also needs the _____ of _____."

6. Look at Exodus 34:28 to see someone else who fasted as Jesus

    did. It was _____.

READ: MATTHEW 4:5-7, LUKE 4:9-12

Satan is always looking for ways to tempt us as he tempted Jesus. He took Jesus to a high place on the temple in Jerusalem.

1. From the above readings, the Devil said to Jesus

    "_____! You won't be hurt."

2. The Devil told Jesus _____ would save him. The angels of _____

    would _____ him and his _____ would not dash against

    a _____.

3. What did Jesus say to Satan in Luke 4:12? _____

    _____

11

READ: MATTHEW 4:8-10, LUKE 4:5-8

Riches and power are things that men of the world desire.

1. Satan took Jesus to a high _____.

2. He offered him _____ and _____.

3. All he had to do to get these things was to _____ Satan.

4. Was Jesus tempted? _____ What did he tell Satan in Matthew 4:10?

_____

_____

READ: MATTHEW 4:11, LUKE 4:13

Satan must have been discouraged as he was not able to win Jesus over by his bribing and dishonest ways.

1. In the above verses, we find at the end of these temptations,

_____ went away.

2. Who came to take care of Jesus? _____

3. We are tempted by Satan even as Jesus was. What are some ways we are tempted?

_____   _____

_____   _____

_____   _____

As we study and learn about Jesus, we will see many examples we can follow.

Matthew 4:17 tells us that Jesus began to preach and teach. This was his mission on earth, to tell us what God wanted us to do to have a good life here and a heavenly home where we can live forever. In this verse he told everyone
"_____

_____."

Think about this statement Jesus made and we will discuss it in class.

JESUS AND THE 12 APOSTLES

MEMORY VERSE: Name the 12 Apostles (Look for them in Matthew 10:2-4)

Jesus could not accomplish everything he wanted to alone. So, he picked twelve special men to help him. These men were not necessarily scholars, doctors, or rich, in fact they were ordinary men who earned their living by hard work. Jesus saw something special in each one.

As he chose them and taught them, they were impressed and amazed at Jesus' goodness and his humbleness. They did not always understand what he taught, but later would remember all of these teachings. They did learn humility, kindness, patience, loyalty, and love from being around this great teacher.

What do you think a disciple or an apostle is? Write down in your own words what you think they are. _____

_____

We will discuss this further during our class time.

From the scriptures we can learn the background of some of these special men.

READ: MATTHEW 4:18-22

1. The apostles (disciples) named here are _____ and _____; and also _____ and _____.

2. They were at the Sea of _____ and were _____.

3. The father of James and John was _____.

4. Jesus told them he would make them _____ of _____.

READ: MATTHEW 9:9

1. The apostle called here was _____.

2. What was his occupation? _____

READ: LUKE 9:1-6

Jesus gave special teachings and power to the apostles.

1. Vs. 2 tells us he gave them power to_____ and to _____the sick.

2. Read vs. 3 and tell what they were to pack in their suitcase. _____

3. Vs. 5 tells us they would not always be welcome in the cities where they were to teach. If they were not listened to or received, they were to _____ the _____ from their _____ as they left.

4. Vs. 6 tells us if they were obedient to Jesus' instructions. Were they? _____ What did they do? _____

There were also others chosen and sent out to help teach. Remember, there were no radios, no TVs, no automobiles, no trains or airplanes. These men walked, or perhaps rode donkeys or camels.

READ: LUKE 10:1, 3, 5, 8-9

1. How many additional men were appointed and sent out? _____

2. How were they to go and where? _____

3. Read vs. 3. What does this mean? _____

   _____

4. What greeting were they to give to each house? (Vs. 5) _____

   _____

5. How were they to get food? (Vs. 8) _____

6. What was their job in each city? (Vs. 9) _____

As we go further in our study of Jesus life, we will see one apostle who did something very bad. Can you guess who it is? _____ Can you find a verse that tells his name? _____

READ: ACTS 1:23-26

1. Who took Judas place as one of the 12 apostles? _____

We will see more and more how important the job of the apostles was. We will find they were loved and hated. They were threatened and some gave their life to carry out their mission given to them by Jesus himself.

We also have a mission to carry out—given by Jesus. Our mission is to save ourselves and then to help others learn about Jesus. We can do this through our example, through teaching others about Jesus, by giving our money to help missionaries teach in other places, and other ways. In order to be able to teach others and save ourselves, we will need to study God's word each day. While Jesus gave instructions personally to the apostles, our instructions are in the Bible.

JESUS LOVED US AND WE MUST LOVE AND CARE ABOUT EACH OTHER.

MIRACLES OF JESUS

MEMORY VERSE: Matthew 11:1

A miracle is a sign; used only on necessary occasions. Jesus used miracles to teach and to support his claim of being God's son. There were miracles during Moses and Joshua's time—remember the people crossing the Red Sea and the Jordan River on dry land and remember how they were fed each day as the manna and quail appeared.

There seems to have been more miracles performed during Jesus time on earth than any other period of Bible history. We will briefly study some of the miracles of Jesus in the next two weeks.

READ-JOHN 2:1-11

1. This was Jesus first miracle. Tell about it.

   _____

   _____

2. Jesus attended the wedding with his _____ and _____

3. What were the containers called? _____

4. How do we know this was Jesus first miracle? (Read vs. 11) _____

   _____

READ: MATTHEW 14:13-21

1. A great _____ of people followed Jesus.

2. The disciples wanted to send the people away in the _____ because they were _____ and it was time to _____.

3. The disciples were concerned because all the food they could find was ____ loaves of bread and _____ _____.

4. Before the food was passed, Jesus _____.

5. Was he able to feed all the people? _____ How many people were there? _____

READ: From MARK 6; the same miracle is written about.

1. Vs. 38 also tells how many loaves _____ and how many fish

   _____ were available to feed the people.

2. Vs. 44 tells us how many were fed. _____

3. Was there enough food for everyone? _____ What does vs. 43 say?

   _____

READ — From LUKE 9; the same miracle is again written about.

1. Vs. 11 tells us two things Jesus did for the people who followed him.

   a. _____

   b. _____

READ: JOHN 6

1. Vs. 9 tells us where the loaves and fishes came from. What does it say?

   _____

2. In vs. 14, we read a statement made by the men who saw this miracle.

   "This is of a _____ that _____ that should come into the

   world."

During our class time we will review this miracle from the information you have just filled in above that came from all four gospels.

Listed below are scriptures describing several miracles that Jesus performed. Pick one, read about it, then write about it below.

Luke 5:12-14

Mark 8:22-26

Matthew 8:23-27

Matthew 14:24-26

John 21:5-11

Scripture: _____ This miracle is about _____

_____

_____

One disciple cried out. "A ghost!" he shouted. When the other disciples looked, they saw a man walking on the water towards them. "Don't be afraid, it is I," a voice shouted above the roaring wind. The voice sounded like Jesus. But was it?

MIRACLES OF JESUS, PART II

MEMORY VERSE — John 9:30

Review the names of the apostles.

READ: John 9: 30-33

1. Why miracles? Read verse 33 again and state the purpose of miracles.

_____

(Look back at the beginning of last week's lesson to help you answer this

question).

SOME OF JESUS MIRACLES WERE TO SHOW HIS POWER THROUGH HEALING.

READ: Luke 17:11-19

1. What was wrong with these men? _____

2. Jesus was on his way to _____ passing through

   _____ and _____. (Vs. 11)

3. These men ask something of Jesus in verse 13, what?

   _____

   _____ What did

   this mean?

   _____

   _____

4. In verse 14, the men were to do an act and as they did it something hap-

   pened. The act was "_____ " and as they went they

   were cleansed.

5. Vs. 15-17 tells us that _____ man turned back to give _____ and

   _____ God. How many were healed?

   _____ And how many thought to be thankful? _____

6. What is leprosy? _____

READ: John 9:1-11

1. This miracle concerns Jesus and a man who was _____ from his birth.

2. Some of the disciples wondered if this condition was caused by _____ of his _____ . (Vs. 2)

3. in verse 3, Jesus said it was not from _____ of the man or his parents but was to accomplish a _____ of God.

4. In the first part of verse 4, Jesus said he was to "_____ the _____ of him who sent me." Who sent him? _____ In verse 5 he also states that he is the _____ of the world.

5. How did Jesus make the blind man see? (Vs. 6-7, 11)

   _____

   _____

6. In verse 8 there were some surprised people over this miracle. They were the man's _____.

7. When the man was blind, how did he make his living? (Vs. 8)

   _____

8. Read verse 38 and see what the blind man said and did.

   _____

READ: John 4:46-54

1. Vs. 54 tells us this was the _____ miracle Jesus performed. The first was at the wedding feast where the _____ was turned into _____.

2. Jesus was visiting in _____ of _____.

3. There was a nobleman whose _____ was sick.

4. The nobleman asked Jesus to come and _____ his son or he would _____.

5. Vs. 50 tells us Jesus told him his son would _____. Did the

nobleman believe what Jesus said? _____ How do you know?

_____

6. In verse 53 the father knew his son was made well the same

_____ when Jesus spoke to him. He and all his household

_____.

In last week's lesson we said a miracle was a sign used only on necessary occasions. As we studied these miracles we can see these signs not only showed Jesus power but caused people to believe.

We need to remember to be thankful for our blessings as the one leper was. God gives us many blessings each day. The leper, the blind man, and the nobleman all were thankful and believed in Jesus because of these wonderful works he performed.

JESUS' MINISTRY

MEMORY VERSE: Matthew 4:17

Jesus was born in Bethlehem of the virgin Mary, and the physical man came into being. But, Jesus spirit had existed long before this.

READ: John 1:1-3

In this reading Jesus is referred to as the Word.

1. The Word (Jesus) was there in the _____.

2. He was with _____ and the same as _____. In other words, Jesus and God are the same and Jesus was with God at the creation of the world. Genesis 1:1 "In the beginning..."

3. We know Jesus was there to help create or make the world because verse 3 tells us "_____ things were made by _____."

READ: Matthew 4:23-25

1. Jesus traveled from place to place teaching. Some of the places were_____, _____, _____. and _____.

2. Jesus taught in the meeting place called the _____. Do you know what a synagogue is?_____

3. Verse 24 tells us Jesus was _____ and many _____ came to hear him and to be _____.

MATTHEW 5

This chapter contains a wonderful sermon taught by Jesus. It is referred to as "The sermon on the mount."

1. Verse 1 tells us Jesus went up into a _____ with his

_____.

2. Verse 3. Blessed are the poor in spirit for theirs is the _____ of heaven. We will discuss "poor in spirit."

_____

3. Verse 7. Blessed are the merciful for they shall obtain _____. We will discuss "merciful." _____

4. Verse 8. Blessed are the pure in heart for they shall see _____. We will discuss "pure in heart." _____

READ: Matthew 5:14-16

1. Who is Jesus talking to when he says we are the light of the world?

_____

2. How do we let our light shine before the world? _____

3. Who will be glorified through our good works? _____

READ: Matthew 5:34-37

Jesus gives us instructions about our speech and swearing or using bad language.

Notice, we aren't to use God's creations to swear by (heaven, earth, etc). Verse 37 gives us specific instructions. We will discuss this in class.

_____

_____

Jesus taught some lessons by parables. Next week we will learn what a parable is and study some of the parables Jesus taught.

JESUS TEACHES IN PARABLES

MEMORY VERSE: Matthew 18:11

READ: Luke 10:27-37

Jesus sometimes told stories or parables to help people understand better what he was trying to teach. This parable is often called "The Parable of the Good Samaritan." Jesus was trying to explain to a certain lawyer about loving your neighbor.

1. In vs. 27 it states to love _____ first and most, then love your neighbor, and last _____

2. The story goes: a certain man was traveling from _____ to _____ when something terrible happened to him. What happened? _____

   _____

3. What was the man's physical condition? _____

4. Well, a priest was coming along the road. Good, surely he would help. What happened? _____

5. Here comes a Levite; he's stopping to look, will he help? _____ What did he do? _____

6. Someone else is coming: a Samaritan man. He won't help, will he. The Samaritan people were not liked very much by the Jews and were not treated very well by them. But wait! The scripture says in vs. 33 that he saw him and had _____ on him.

7. What did he do then? _____

8. Where did he take the wounded man? _____ He also paid _____ for his keep.

9. Vs. 36 Jesus asks a question, "Which one was the neighbor?" Who do you think was the neighbor? _____

Jesus is telling us to love our neighbors which are all those around us. We love each other by caring and helping. When we do this we are doing Christian works.

READ: Matthew 18:11-14

1. This parable is about _____.

2. Is every sheep important to a shepherd? _____

3. The story says, the shepherd has _____ sheep but _____ sheep became lost.

4. What does the shepherd do?_____

5. When the lost sheep is found, the shepherd _____.

Even though this story is about sheep, it really is about people. Jesus is telling us that each person is very important to God. Vs. 14 tells us that God doesn't want even _____ person to be lost.

We should encourage each other and everyone around us to be a Christian. God doesn't want anyone to be lost and we are God's helpers here on this earth.

"The shepherd left the ninety-nine sheep, and went out to look for the one that was lost. He hunted every-where for that one lost sheep. When he finally found it he was full of joy. Gently he put the little sheep on his shoulders and carried it home.

ANOTHER PARABLE, ABOUT TALENTS

MEMORY VERSE — Matthew 5:16

READ: Matthew 25:14-30

Read this passage through more than once. Be looking for things these people did right, and things you think they may have done better than they did. Notice Jesus' teachings as you read.

We will consider this reading during our class time as it relates to:

1. Money _____

_____

_____

2. Abilities _____

_____

_____

3. Rewards _____

_____

_____

REVIEW your Apostles names.

The names of the apostles are like a stamp with J's at the corners and a B in the middle; but you have to spell it "STTAMPP"

_____   _____

STTAMPP

_____   _____

_____   _____

_____   _____

_____   _____

We can call this a post**Mark**. Where are the apostle's names found in the book of Mark? _____ (Chapter & verse)

JESUS TEACHES TRUST IN GOD

MEMORY VERSE: Luke 12:31

A great multitude gathered and Jesus taught the disciples about trusting in God and God's care.

READ: Luke 12:13-21

1. Jesus taught here that a man's life does not depend on how much he

    _____ (vs. 15)

2. Jesus teaches the disciples a lesson by a _____.

3. The rich man had so much that his _____ would not hold it. He

    planned to _____ these and build _____

    ones. (vs. 18)

4. Vs. 19 tells us he was quite proud of himself. He decided he would cele-

    brate, how? _____

5. God was not pleased with the man. Read vs. 20-21. God called him a

    _____. He would _____ and his treasures would

    mean nothing to him.

READ: Luke 12:22-30

1. Jesus tells us not to worry about our _____ and _____.

    (vs.22)

2. In vs. 23 he says life is more important than what we _____ or what

    we _____

3. Two examples were used by Jesus in vs. 24-27. They are the

    _____ which is a _____, and the _____

    which are _____.

4. Tell about the raven. _____

5. Tell about the lilies. _____

6. These stories were told by Jesus to explain God's care. In vs. 28-30 Jesus tells us that the Father (God) knows that we have _____. We are not to worry because He will _____ and _____ us.

7. in vs. 28, Jesus teaches one very important thing: we are to have

_____

READ: Luke 12:31

All of the things we have studied today about God's care are there in the Bible for us to know how to set our priorities. Do you know what that means?

1. In vs. 31, he tells what is the most important thing. What does it tell you?

_____

_____

READ: Matthew 6:19-21

1. If our earthly treasures are all that is important, what will happen to them?

_____

2. What do you think are the treasures we lay up (or store) in Heaven?

_____

2. What happens to these treasures? _____

3. How will God know what kind of person we are? (vs. 21)

_____

PRAYER

We will just review a few things about prayer that might be a help to the boys leading prayer in class... and we just might learn a little more about prayer too.

First — How does God talk to us? _____

Then — How do we talk to Him? _____

Okay, let's look up a few scriptures to be sure we talk to Him, or pray in a manner that God accepts.

Matthew 21:22 And all things you ask in prayer, believing, you will receive.

When we ask God to help us or to help someone, or we ask for anything we need, we need to ask, believing that He will give it to us. Of course we know, depending on the thing we ask for, God may say Yes, No, or maybe Wait. But, would there be any reason to pray if we did not believe God would hear us and help us?

Ephesians 3:14 For this reason I bow my knee before the Father...

We do not have to bow down on our knees to pray, even though in my early years in the church, when men prayed, they bowed on one knee. This shows a reverence for God, our awesome God. As we bow our heads this morning, we show our reverence and also by keeping our minds on the words spoken.

Ephesians 5:20 Giving thanks for all things in the name of our Lord Jesus Christ to God even the Father.

Have you noticed men, and even boys in our class, praying in Jesus name? They are doing this because the Bible teaches through this scripture to pray in Jesus' name. Jesus is sitting at the right hand of God and intercedes for us by helping us send our message to God.(Rom. 8:34) Sometimes we don't know just how to word our prayer but Jesus is there to help us send a beautiful prayer to God. So remember boys, we pray "In Jesus Name."

JESUS TEACHES ABOUT FORGIVENESS

MEMORY VERSE: Luke 15:10

<u>**READ: Luke 15:11-12**</u>

Jesus tells a story, and from this story we can learn about forgiveness.

1. In this story Jesus is telling us about a _____ and his _____ _____.

2. One son, he was the _____ one, decided he wanted his part of the inheritance from his father. (Vs. 12)

3. Did his father give it to him? _____ (Vs. 12)

4. Then what did the younger son do? (Vs. 13) _____

_____

5. After a while there was a _____ in the land. (Vs. 14) This means there wasn't enough _____.

6. Vs. 15-17. This young man became a keeper of _____. He became so hungry he wanted to eat _____ the same as the _____.

7. Vs. 17 tells us the young man came to himself. He remembered things about home. What were these things? _____

8. Vs. 18 tells us he decided to go _____.

9. As he arrived home, his father's reaction was what? _____. How do you know? _____ (Vs. 20-23)

10. But, the son said he was not _____ to be called his son because he had sinned against the father and against _____ (Vs. 21)

11. The father was so happy to see his son. He had not known if he was _____ or _____ and the _____ was now _____. (Vs. 24)

There was an elder (older) son in the household. Let's see what his reaction is to his brothers return. Is he as happy about this situation as the father?

12. Where was the older son when all of this was happening? (Vs. 25)

_____

13. He knew something was going on because he heard _____ and

_____. (Vs. 25)

14. What did the servant tell him was happening? (Vs. 27) _____

_____ -

15. And how did he react? (Vs. 28) _____

16. He had a talk with his father. In vs. 29 he told his father he had _____

him many years. He had not _____ him. And in vs. 29, he

reminded his father that he had never given him a _____

or let him make _____

with his friends.

The older son could not understand why his brother, who had done bad things and squandered all his inheritance and now had come back home with nothing, was being treated so well by his father, while he had stayed home and worked hard and nothing had been done for him.

The father explained that he loved both of them and knew he was faithful and dependable, but they should rejoice because the younger brother had been lost and was now home again. (Vs. 32)

Sometimes Christians become discouraged and unfaithful. They don't pray, or attend worship services. They transgress against God as this younger son did. Then they come to themselves as he did (repent) and return to the church. All of us who are in the church and faithful as the elder son was, should rejoice and welcome them back. We should also be happy that we have remained faithful and now can encourage the wayward Christian who has returned.

SOME QUESTIONS ASKED OF JESUS

There were some lawyers, scribes and Pharisees who asked questions of Jesus. READ: Mark 12:28-31

1. A scribe asked Jesus, "Which is the first _____?" (Vs. 28)

2. Jesus answered in vs. 30. Write down what he said.

   _____

   _____

   _____

3. And what did Jesus tell him was the second commandment? (Vs. 31)

   _____

   _____

READ: Matthew 22:15-21 (Also recorded in Luke 20:20-40)

1. This time Jesus was asking a question by a _____. (Vs. 15)

2. First they flattered Jesus by saying they knew he would tell the _____. (Vs. 16) But Jesus knew their hearts and called them _____. Do you know what a hypocrite is? _____

3. The question was concerning_____. Should they pay _____ to _____ or not? (Vs. 17)

4. Jesus asked them to show him the _____. (Vs. 19) He called their attention to the image on the coin. It was the image of _____ . (Vs.20-21)

5. Read vs. 21 — Did Jesus say pay tribute to Caesar or not? _____ And what about God? _____

They were talking about paying taxes to the government (Caesar), the same as your parents pay taxes today. Is this a right thing to do? We will discuss this more in class.

READ: Luke 11:1-4

1. This request was made by one of Jesus' _____. The re-

quest was "_____"

This prayer is sometimes called "The Lord's Prayer." We will discuss this prayer in class.

READ: Luke 11:9-10

These are Jesus' words concerning prayer. What do you think this means?

_____

_____

If you have studied your lesson this far, good for you!! Now you may pick a verse from the third section of your lesson for your memory verse.

CHARACTERISTICS OF JESUS

MEMORY VERSE: John 11:35

What kind of person was Jesus? When we read about Jesus as he was here on earth, we see examples and teachings on how we should live.

READ: Matthew 19:13-15

What does this reading tell you about Jesus? _____

READ: Luke 2:41 & 51

What does this reading tell you about Jesus? _____

READ: Matthew 5:44

What is Jesus teaching in this reading? _____

_____

READ: John 11:1, 3, 14, 32-35

What does this reading tell you about Jesus? _____

READ: Matthew 18: 21-22

What do we learn about Jesus in this reading? _____

READ: Matthew 14:13-14

What does this reading tell us about Jesus? _____

_____

READ: John 15:13

What does this reading tell us about Jesus? _____

READ: Matthew 12:10-15

What does this reading tell us about Jesus? _____

_____

From what you have studied, list some of the characteristics of Jesus.

_____   _____

_____   _____

_____   _____

_____   _____

Are these characteristics that could be and should be in your life?

Was Jesus ever angry? _____ Can you find a scripture that supports your answer?

_____

A REVIEW

MEMORY VERSE: Be able to name the 12 Apostles

Let's take a brief review of what we have studied from the gospels. We will soon go into a study of Jesus' last days on earth. We want to remember Bible facts on where Jesus came from, what he taught, and the examples he set.

If you have kept up on your lessons it will be easy for you to answer the questions on this review. Even if you need to look them up, please try to answer each one.

LESSON 1 (Birth)

1. If someone asks you where in the Bible to look for

    information on Jesus' life, where would you tell them to look?

    _____, _____, _____, and _____.

    These books are called the _____

2. John was a special man. He was a cousin to Jesus. His mission was to help

    prepare for the coming of _____

3. Jesus' mother was _____ and his earthly father was

    _____.

4. There was much interest shown when Jesus was born. A _____ shone

    brightly in the _____. _____ saw it as they watched their

    sheep in the fields. Wise men also came to see Jesus. How many wise men

    came to see Jesus? _____

LESSON 2 (Boyhood)

1. Jesus went to Jerusalem with his parents when he was _____ years old.

2. Jesus became "lost" from his family for _____ days. He was found in

    the temple with _____. He said he was "_____

    _____ "

3. He went home to _____ with his family and was _____

    to them.

LESSON 3 (Baptism)

1. _____ baptized Jesus in the _____ River. Jesus was baptized to teach obedience to God, not because of sin. Jesus had no _____.

2. How did John die? _____

LESSON 4 (Temptations)

1. Jesus did not eat for _____ days.

2. Name one of the temptations Satan offered to Jesus _____
_____

3. Did Jesus give in to Satan? _____

LESSON 5 (Apostles)

1. Name two brothers who were Apostles. _____ and
_____.

2. Some of these men were _____.

3. How many Apostles were there? _____

4. Which one do you think of when you hear "I doubt it"?_____

LESSON 6 (Miracles)

1. What was Jesus' first miracle? _____
Where was it performed? _____

2. Jesus fed _____ men plus women and children from a little lad's lunch of _____ loaves and _____ fish. Did everyone eat? _____ Anything left over? _____

LESSON 7 (Miracles)

1. What is the purpose of a miracle? Why did Jesus perform them? _____
_____

2. When Jesus healed _____ lepers, how many came back to thank him?
_____

3. Jesus second miracle was the healing of the nobleman's _____.

LESSON 8 (Ministry)

1. In this lesson we learn Jesus was with _____ even from the beginning, when the heavens and _____ were created.

2. In Jesus' teachings we learn we must be "poor in _____", "_____ in heart" and "mer_____."

3. Jesus taught in G_____, J_____, and J_____

4. What does the Bible tell us about our language? _____

LESSON 9 (Parable)

1. Put these in proper order. We should love _____ first, then your _____ and last _____.

2. Which of these men was a good neighbor to the traveling man and why?

   _____

LESSON 10 (Talents)

1. The lesson on talents teaches us to do the very _____ we can with what _____ God has blesses us with.

LESSON 11 (Trust)

1. What two examples were used to teach us that God will take care of our needs? _____ and _____

2. We learned it was more important to lay up our treasures in _____ rather than here on earth where thieves _____ and things spoil.

LESSON 12 (Forgiveness)

1. We can learn about forgiveness from the story of a man who had _____ sons.

2. One son _____ all his inheritance and then came home broke and _____

39

3. The other son stayed at home and obeyed his father but was not willing to

_____ his brother's wrongs.

4. The father loved them both, but was so happy to have his son who was

_____ back home. The father's forgiveness of his younger son

is a good example for us.

LESSON 13 (Questions)

1. Four things we learned from the Lord's model prayer in Luke 11 were:

a. _____

b. _____

c. _____

d. _____

2. Underline the correct answer. Jesus told the Pharisees it (was, was not) al-

right to pay taxes to Caesar.

3. When we pray we should ask for things we _____, thank

God for things we _____ and pray _____.

LESSON 14 (Characteristics)

1. Name some characteristics we learned about Jesus in this lesson.

a. _____

b. _____

c. _____

d. _____

We are studying in the NEW TESTAMENT

1. There are _____ books in the NEW TESTAMENT.

2. The Gospels are _____ , _____ , _____ , and

_____

3. The Gospels tell us of Jesus' _____ , _____ , and

_____.

4. There are _____ writers of the NEW TESTAMENT.

5. The writers are _____, _____, _____,

_____, _____, _____, _____, and

_____.

JESUS PREPARES HIS DISCIPLES

MEMORY VERSE: Luke 9:25

In three of the gospels we read how Jesus tried to prepare his followers for what was to happen to him in the near future. We also can note how they did not understand or really think these things could happen to Jesus—their friend, a kind and caring man, a man they loved so much.

READ — Matthew 16:21-28

1. Jesus must go into the city of _____ (vs. 21) where these things would take place.

2. Name three things he said would happen, (vs. 21)

    a. _____

    b. _____

    c. _____

3. In vs. 22 and 23, who did not believe these things would really happen? _____ Jesus said to him, "Get _____ _____ _____ Satan, thou art an _____ to me."

4. If we follow Jesus, we must _____ ourselves, take up His _____ and follow Him. (vs. 24)

5. If we are only interested in things of this world, we can lose our _____. (vs.26) What is your soul worth? Jesus asked His disciples what they would exchange for their soul.

    _____

6. Vs. 27 tells us Jesus will come a second time and _____ every man according to his works.

READ: Mark 8:31

1. Mark writes the same as Matthew about Jesus' coming death. What three things does he write that Jesus says will happen to Him?

    _____, _____, _____.

42

READ: Luke 9:22-27

1. Does Luke hear Jesus say the same things as Matthew and Mark in vs. 22? _____

2. In vs. 23 Luke quotes Jesus as saying we must _____ ourselves and follow _____.

3. Read vs. 24 and 25. Do you know what this means? Discuss with your parents or an adult in your home. We will also discuss in class.

4. If we are ashamed of Jesus and His teachings, how will Jesus feel about us before his Father (God) and the Angels? (vs. 26)

   _____

Jesus makes a statement in Matthew 16:28, Mark 9:1, and Luke 9:27 about the kingdom and death. Do you understand these verses—keep in mind that the "kingdom" is the church which Jesus will purchase with His blood when he dies on the cross. Does this help you to understand His statement? We will discuss these verses in class, but be prepared to discuss them.

THE TRANSFIGURATION

MEMORY VERSE: Luke 9:35

A few days after Jesus talked to His disciples about His coming suffering and death, a very special and unusual thing happened before the eyes of three of the Apostles. It was a beautiful and wonderful experience for them, and also for us to read about. Don't let the word "transfiguration" confuse you; it means "changed".

READ: Matthew 17:1-9

1. Name the three Apostles present. (Vs. 1) _____,

   _____, and _____.

2. Jesus was transfigured or _____ before these men. What

   happened? (Vs. 2) _____

   _____

3. Some men from times past appeared. Who were they? (Vs. 3) _____

   and _____.

4. In vs. 5 something else happened. Tell about it. _____

   _____

5. How did the disciples react? _____

   (vs. 6) But Jesus comforted them, how? _____

   (vs. 7)

6. We know Moses and Elias was a vision because they _____

   (vs. 8)

7. In vs. 9 Jesus asked them to do something. What? _____

   _____

READ: Mark 9:2-10

You found almost the same description as in Matthew didn't you? Just one or two additional pieces of information for you.

1. Vs. 5 tells us Peter wanted to do something special to mark the occasion.

   What was it? _____

2. In vs. 7 God speaks, telling Peter who is the important one on this occasion.

Tell in your own words what he says to Peter. _____

_____

3.   In vs. 9 Jesus tells them to keep these things to themselves until a certain

time. What time was this?

_____

READ: Luke 9:28-36
1.   Another additional bit of information about the transfiguration is told in vs.

32. What is it? _____

2.   How did God appear to the Apostles when He spoke of Jesus as His beloved

son? _____ He told them to _____

Him. (Vs. 35)

This seems rather mysterious to us doesn't it? But it got the attention of the
three Apostles, as it does ours too. Jesus and God tell us about Jesus as God's special Son to whom we are to listen, and also about his forthcoming special sacrifice
for us.

A riddle:
LPOGSE = GOOD NEWS

DO YOU KNOW ABOUT THESE MEN —
The Twelve Apostles

1. How many were fishermen, that we know of? _____

2. One was a tax collector, he was _____

3. There were two sets of brothers, they were

   _____ and _____

   _____ and _____

4. One of them was called a zealot (that is sort of a rebel). Do you know what his name was? _____

5. Two had the same name. Their name was _____.

6. One did bad things, he destroyed himself. His name was

   _____.

7. One has a longer name, begins with the second letter of the alphabet and is spelled exactly like it is sounded out _____.

8. There were two T's, name them. _____ and

   _____

9. There were also two P's. They were _____ and _____.

10. Do you remember what Peter's first name was? There was an apostle by this name. _____

11. Now you have named all 12 of them in the statements above; list them below.

   _____

   _____

   _____

   _____

EVENTS OF JESUS' LAST WEEK ON EARTH

MEMORY VERSE: You will be expected to write the names of the 12 Apostles.

As Jesus enters the last week of His life on this earth, there are certain events we want to study.

Jesus Enters Jerusalem

READ: Mark 11:1-9 and Luke 19: 29-38

1. Jesus sent two of his disciples to do a job. They were in the area near the Mount of Olives. In what verse do you find this information?

   _____

2. They were to go into a village and find a colt tied up and were to bring it back. In what verse is this found? _____

3. What was unusual about the colt? _____

4. In what verse does it say 'someone might question them'?_____

5. What were they to answer if questioned? (Luke 19:34, Mark 11:3)

   _____

6. What did they do with the colt? (Mark 11:7 and Luke 19:35).

   _____

7. In Mark 11:8, what did the people do as Jesus rode the colt into Jerusalem? _____

8. Mark 11:9 and Luke 19:37-38 tells us the people's reaction as Jesus came. What did they do?

   _____

   _____

Do you remember why the Jews celebrated the Passover Feast? Think back to when they were slaves in Egypt. Remember Moses asked Pharaoh to let them go but he would not. Them God sent 10 plagues to try to convince him to let the people go. Can you remember what the 10th plague was?

Jesus observes the Passover Feast with his Disciples

READ: Mark 14:12-26 and Matthew 26:17-30

1. In Mark 14:12-16 and Matthew 26:17-19, we are given information about the place and the people involved. Write in your words what happened.

   _____

   _____

2. What time of day did Jesus come and meet with his 12 Apostles?

   _____ (Mark 14:17)

3. As Jesus ate the Passover Feast with His Apostles, what did he talk to them about? (Matt. 26:21-23 and Mark 14:18-20)

   _____

   _____

4. The bread He used at this supper was to represent His _____ and the cup was to represent His _____. (Mark 14:23-24)

5. Jesus talked about the Apostle who would betray Him. Who would this be? _____ (John 13:26-27) What warning did Jesus give to this person? _____

6. Jesus stated in Matthew 26:29 and Mark 14:25 when He would again eat this supper. When would it be? _____

7. Before they departed the house, what did they do and where did they go when they left the house? (Mark 14:26) a. _____ b.

   _____

READ — Mark 14:1-2 and Matthew 26:3-5

As Jesus is planning and having the Passover Feast with His Apostles, there were other things going on. As you read the above scriptures, what do you learn was being planned concerning Jesus?

_____

READ: John 13:1

Did Jesus know He was going to die? _____ Jesus did this for mankind

because He _____ them and also for us today.

Today, Christians are remembering Jesus as He ate this feast with His Apostles, how He died on the cross for us and how He is in Heaven waiting for us, What do they do to observe or remember these things Jesus taught? Today, in worship, can you think on these things we have talked about?

JESUS' ARREST AND TRIAL

MEMORY VERSE: Matthew 26:35

After the Passover supper, Jesus went into the Garden of Gethsemane on the Mount of Olives.

READ: Luke 22:39-46

1. Jesus went into the garden to _____. (vs. 41)

2. Read verse 42, How did Jesus feel about giving up His life? _____

    _____

3. God sent help to Jesus as He prayed. What was this help? (vs. 43)

    _____

4. Jesus was praying so earnestly during this time that a strange thing happened to Him. Can you find it in this reading? (vs. 44) _____

5. Jesus had asked the disciples to wait as He went alone to pray. He had told them to watch and pray, but when He returned to them, what were they doing? _____ (vs. 45)

READ: Matthew 26:47-49

1. Jesus was betrayed. By whom and how? _____

    _____

READ: Matthew 26:31 -35

1. What did Jesus say the disciples would do when He, the Shepherd, was taken? (vs. 31) _____

2. What did Peter say in vs. 35? _____

    _____

READ: Matthew 26:56

1. As Jesus was arrested what did His disciples do? _____

READ — Matthew 26:69-75

1. What did Peter do? _____

    Jesus was arrested and brought before the politicians of that day, the chief priests, elders, Pontius Pilate and Caiaphas the high priest

1. What were their plans for Jesus? (Matthew 27:1) _____

2. How did they treat Jesus? (Matthew 27:29-30) _____

   _____

3. As Jesus went before Pilate to be judged, what did the people say to Pilate? (John 19:5-6) _____

4. Read Matthew 27:31-35. Describe what happened to Jesus here. _____

   _____

Most criminals are arrested and brought to trial for a criminal act: they have broken the law and committed some bad thing. Jesus was a kind, compassionate person who had performed miracles of healing, was friendly to everyone, and concerned about everyone. What terrible crime was he arrested for?

JESUS' GREAT SACRIFICE

MEMORY VERSE: Luke 23:34

READ: John 19:17-19

Write a short description of what you have read _____

_____

_____

READ: Matthew 27:46

What does Jesus say as He hangs on the cross? _____

_____

READ: Matthew 27:45

What happened at this time? _____

_____

READ: Matthew 27:50

We see that Jesus dies as He hangs on the cross. In verses 51, 52, and 53 there were unusual things happening. Name some of them:

1) _____

2) _____

3) _____

READ: Matthew 27:57-60

What happened to Jesus' body? _____

READ: Matthew 27:64-66

Those who condemned Jesus to death were concerned over some statements He had made about rising in 3 days. What did they do to be sure He couldn't get out of the grave?

_____

READ: Luke 24:1-8

What wonderful thing has happened? _____

_____

Scriptures of interest to read before class:
John 20:30-31; John 21:25

Jesus has appeared to His followers on a number of occasions after He was risen from the dead. We can find out the "rest of the story" by reading Acts 1:9-11. Let's be ready to discuss this reading in our class time.

This concludes our study of the gospels; Matthew, Mark, Luke and John. We have covered just a small portion of all of these books. We have talked about how they fit together, not contradicting each other but in some instances telling the exact same things, and in other instances adding a bit more information. The writers of these books were directed by god as they wrote what they had seen and heard.

What a wonderful thing that we have written down for us to study the life of Jesus our savior. Hopefully we have become better acquainted with Jesus—that we know him better because of these books—and we can see the great sacrifice he endured for us to have our sins forgiven and be able to look forward to our home in heaven where we will see and talk to him.

As young people you will be making a decision each day whether you will live for Jesus and plan your goal toward heaven. Study your bible. Don't let anything keep you from learning about the wonderful life of a Christian. After all, eternity is longer than we can imagine, and we will be so happy there.

ACTS

NAME THE TWELVE APOSTLES—AFTER JUDAS KILLED HIMSELF.

1. _____
2. _____
3. _____
4. _____
5. _____
6. _____
7. _____
8. _____
9. _____
10. _____
11. _____
12. _____

LOOK UP THE THREE AGES OF TIME IN YOUR BIBLE FACT SHEET AND WRITE THEM DOWN.

1. _____
2. _____
3. _____

CAN YOU WRITE THE FIRST SENTENCE IN THE BIBLE? (GENESIS 1:1)

_____

_____

IN HOW MANY DAYS DID GOD CREATE THE HEAVENS AND THE EARTH?

_____ DAYS

WHAT RELIGIOUS HOLIDAY WERE THE JEWS CELEBRATING WHEN JESUS WAS CRUCIFIED?

_____

FOUR OF THE APOSTLES WERE FISHERMEN, AND ALSO BROTHERS. CAN YOU NAME THE BROTHERS TOGETHER?

_____ and _____

_____ and _____

FILL IN THE BLANKS....

_____ LOVES ME THIS I KNOW, FOR THE _____ TELLS ME SO.

THE FIRST BOOK IN THE BIBLE IS _____ AND THE LAST ONE IS _____.

FOR _____ SO LOVED THE WORLD THAT HE GAVE HIS ONLY BE-GOTTEN _____ THAT WE SHOULD NOT PERISH BUT HAVE EV-ERLASTING LIFE (John 3:16).

HOW LONG IS ETERNITY? _____

JESUS PREPARES THE DISCIPLES FOR THE CHURCH

During the last part of Jesus' life on earth, He revealed many things to his close followers. One of his statements will be your memory verse — Matthew 16:18.

MATTHEW 13

1.   What did Jesus talk to the disciples about? (vs. 11) _____

_____

2.   Did Jesus expect everyone to understand? (vs. 17) _____

_____

3.   How did Jesus tell them about the kingdom of Heaven? (vs. 34) _____

_____

4.   He said that the kingdom was like:

   a.   (v. 24) _____ How? _____

   _____

   b.   (v. 31-32) _____ How? _____

   _____

   c.   (v. 44) _____ How? _____

   _____

   d.   (v 45-46) _____ How? _____

   _____

   e.   (v. 47-48) _____ How? _____

   _____

Doesn't this sound like a very special thing? We know now that it was so special that Christ died for this glorious kingdom, and that we can be part of it!

5.   Why did Jesus speak in parables? (vs. 35) _____

_____

6.   The things that Jesus spoke had been known by God since _____

_____ (vs. 35)

MATTHEW 16

1. In this chapter Jesus had a very important conversation with his disciples. What question did Jesus ask in verse 13? _____

   _____

2. Who answered? (vs. 16) _____ What was his answer? _____

   _____

3. Was Jesus pleased with his answer? (vs. 17) _____

   _____

4. Verses 18-19 show us that the kingdom and the _____ are the same. What did Jesus plan to build? _____ Who would the church belong to? _____

5. In verse 19, Jesus is telling Peter that he (Peter) will have some authority in the church. Can you explain this verse? _____

   _____

(We will talk about this in class more: don't worry if you don't completely understand).

Jesus had said, "I will build MY church..." Did Jesus have the authority to do this? In a previous lesson, we learned that God gave Jesus the authority.

6. What was the story? (Matt. 17:2) _____

7. How do we know Jesus had authority? (Matt. 17:5) _____

8. In Matt. 16:28 Jesus tells the disciples something about when Jesus' Church (the kingdom) would be built. How long would it be? _____

   _____

9. Do you think this has already happened? _____

10. Has the church been built? _____

11. Has the kingdom been established? _____

(Future lessons will make this even more evident).

In Matthew 16:21 Jesus told the disciples some other things to expect. And, as we have already learned, all these things DID happen. After Jesus died and was raised He gave the disciples more instructions.

12. In Acts 1:4-5, He asked them to stay in _____ be-

    cause they would soon be baptized with the _____.

13. Acts 2 tells us when and where they were and what happened.

    a. When? (vs. 1) _____

    b. Where? (vs.5) _____

    c. What happened? (vs.4) _____

    _____

14. Then in Acts 2:14 someone began to speak. Who? _____

15. Did Jesus say this would happen? (see 5. above) _____

    a. What chapter and verse? _____

On the day of Pentecost miraculous things happened and Peter preached the first gospel sermon. Many people were there and learned how they could become part of Christ's church. This is how and when the church began. In our next lesson we will study about these early days of the church. Remember, if we are members of Christ's church we belong to His kingdom and will have the things Christ talked about in question #4.

THE CHURCH ESTABLISHED ON PENTECOST

MEMORY VERSE: ACTS 2:38

In our last lesson Peter was about to speak to the multitude of people who were gathered in Jerusalem for the observance of the day of Pentecost. It is important to know that Peter was not just another man who was giving his own opinion. He was speaking under Jesus' authority and under the influence of the Holy Spirit.

Peter's Authority

1. Matthew 16:19. Jesus gave Peter the _____ to the kingdom of Heaven. Jesus told Peter that what he bound on earth would be bound in _____.

2. Matthew 28:16-20. After Jesus was raised from the dead, He met with His disciples and gave them instructions. In verses 19 and 20 Jesus told them three things to do. Fill in the verbs.

    a. _____ to all nations

    b. _____ them in the name of the Father and of the Son and of the Holy Spirit.

    c. _____ them to observe all commandments

3. Acts 2 :1-4. Peter and the other Apostles were waiting in Jerusalem when miraculous things happened, (vs. 4)

    a. They were filled with the _____.

    b. They spoke in _____. (This means they _____ Spirit helped them speak in other languages so the people there could all understand).

The Spirit gave them the Message: Acts 2

4. Vs. 5. Who heard the message? Devout men from every _____

5. Vs. 6. How did they hear it? In their own _____

6. Vs. 11. What was the message about? _____

7. Vs. 12. The different nations of people were amazed and asked,

61

8. Some people said the Apostles must be _____ (vs. 13), but Peter

    explained that they were fulfilling a prophecy from the book of

    _____ (vs. 16).

9. The prophecy told of dreams, and visions, and prophesying and also said

    that God would pour out His _____ (vs. 17) (Holy Spirit) and

    that the people who would call on His name could be _____ (vs.

    21).

  *** This passage starts with God's promise to pour out His Spirit,
and ends with God's promise to save people. *** (Joel 2:28-32)

    Peter told the people all about how Jesus had been:
- Sent to earth by God
- Crucified by the people
- Raised from the dead
- Exalted to the right hand of God

10. Then in verse 36 He reminded them that Jesus was both _____

    and _____ and they were the ones who _____

    Him.

The Question: Acts 2

11. Vs. 37. When they realized what Peter said was true, they were _____

    in their hearts and asked, "_____?"

The Answer: Acts 2

12. Vs. 38-39. Peter answered "_____ and be _____,

    every one of you in the name of _____ for the

    _____ of your _____; and you shall receive

    the gift of the _____."

  These verses refer to a gift and a promise. God has given people many gifts, but
the kind of gift that is referred to here is His promise to allow people to have their

sins forgiven, to be saved, and to be a part of His everlasting kingdom.

The Action: Acts 2

13.   Vs.41. Did anyone believe Peter? _____

14.   What did they do? _____

15.   How many people? _____

16.   This verse says people were "added".

17.   To what were they added? _____

18.   Which ones were added? _____

19.   According to vs. 47, who did the adding? _____

20.   Which ones did He add? _____

* * * Summary — On this day of Pentecost God's Spirit poured out on people. Peter preached what Jesus had asked him to preach, and people were baptized and saved.

Afterward, Peter and others continued to preach to many people in many places and the church continued to grow. Next week we will study about more ways and places the church grew and what the early Christians did.

CHRIST'S CHURCH
REVIEW TEST 1

1. Did Jesus predict the building of a church? _____

    a. What chapter and verse? _____

    b. Who was He talking to? _____

2. The Church is the same as the _____.

3. Was the Church built before or after Jesus' crucifixion? _____

4. Was the Church built before or after Jesus ascended? _____

5. In what town did the Church begin? _____

6. At what Jewish celebration? _____

7. What sort of people were there? _____

8. Who preached to them? _____

9. Which Old Testament prophet did he talk about? _____

10. In what book and chapter is Peter's address? _____

11. What did Peter tell them in Acts 2:36? _____

    _____

12. How did they respond? _____

    _____

13. Copy Acts 2:38. _____

    _____

    _____

14. How many people were baptized? _____

15. How many people were added to the Church? _____

NEW CHRISTIANS

MEMORY VERSE: ACTS 5:42

On the first day of the Church at least 3000 people were saved. In the Acts we also learn what kind of things these first Christians did.

READ: Acts 2:42-47

Acts 2:42 says they were devoted. List 4 things they were devoted to:

1. _____   3. _____

2. _____   4. _____

Vs. 45 tells how they helped each other. What did they do?

_____

_____

_____

Vs. 46. How often did they go to the temple?

_____

Read vs. 46 and 47. In your own words, tell what you think the people were like:

_____

_____

Do you think this is what Jesus had in mind for his Church? _____

READ: Acts 4:32-37

What was their attitude toward personal property? _____

Was anyone there needy? _____ Why not? _____

What did Joseph (Barnabas) do? _____

READ: Acts 5:12-16

The apostles continued to do many _____ and _____ (vs.

12) and they were held in _____ (vs. 13) by the people.

Vs. 14. What happened to the Church? _____

Vs. 15 and 16. What did people from surrounding towns do? _____

_____

    The apostles continued to teach boldly and to heal people and the Church continued to increase. Read Acts 5:42 and tell how they continued to teach.

READ-Acts 6:1-6
1.   Acts 6:1. Tell how their teaching affected the Church. _____

2.   Acts 6:1-6 also tells of the first Church leadership. _____

3.   How many men were chosen? _____

4.   What was their job to be? _____

5.   Why couldn't the apostles have done this? (vs. 4) _____

6.   Throughout Acts, we see the Word being spread and people being converted.

7.   Acts 8:4-6 Who went? _____ To where? _____

    What happened? _____

8.   Acts 8:14 Who went? _____ To where? _____

9.   Other places gained churches. What places? _____

    a. Acts 9:31 _____

    b. 9:32 _____

    c. 11:19-21 _____

    d. 9:36 _____

READ: Acts 11:22-26
1.   What did Barnabas find at Antioch?

    _____

2.   Were the people faithful? _____

    By now churches had been started in many places. The Church at Antioch must have been especially strong. It was good for Barnabas and he was good for them.

3.   What does vs. 24 say about Barnabas? _____

4.   What does it say about the Church? _____

5.   Because of the large number of faithful disciples at Antioch, they came to be

known as _____ (vs. 26). This means they strove to be

_____-like.

In this lesson we see the wonders and miracles of God's word spreading across the land and see thousands of people learning how to become Christians and how to act like Christians. What we have studied so far has not shown any opposition or hardship. In future lessons we will see that things were not easy for these new Christians. They faced many threats and dangers. Some were persecuted even to the death, but they knew that the Kingdom (Church) built by Jesus was worth a great price because Christ himself had died for it.

I. CORINTHIANS, CHAPTER 13

1. ONE WORD IN THIS CHAPTER IS MOST IMPORTANT WHAT IS THAT WORD? _____

2. IN ORDER TO PLEASE GOD, VERSE 4, THERE ARE FOUR THINGS OR WAYS WE MUST DEVELOP. NAME THEM.

    a. _____

    b. _____

    c. _____

    d. _____

3. FILL IN THE BLANKS. If I have the gift of _____, and know all _____ and _____ knowledge; and if I have all _____ so as to _____ mountains, but _____ have _____

4. WHEN I WAS A CHILD, I SPOKE _____, BUT AS A MAN, I PUT AWAY _____ THINGS.

5. LOCATE THESE:

    a. NOISY GONG OR CLANGING CYMBAL. _____

    b. LOVE NEVER FAILS. _____

    c. LOVE IS KIND AND IS NOT JEALOUS. _____

6. NOW _____, FAITH, HOPE, LOVE, BUT THE _____ IS _____.

NOW, CLOSE YOUR BIBLE AND CLOSE YOUR EYES AND SEE HOW MUCH OF THIS CHAPTER YOU STILL CAN REMEMBER.

REMEMBER TO REVIEW IT OFTEN SO YOU WON'T FORGET.

WHEN THE GOING GETS TOUGH....

MEMORY VERSE: ACTS 5:29

When Peter and the apostles stood up and preached on the day of Pentecost, they were not welcome guests! The Pentecost Festival was a part of the Jewish religion and the Jews were there to carry on with their religious ceremonies. So when Peter bravely told them that the Christ had come and died for a new Church, some of them were very disturbed and angry and set out to stop the spread of the Church.

ACTS 4

1. Vs. 1-3. Peter and John continued to preach and to heal and this annoyed the _____ and the captain of the _____. So, what happened to Peter and John? _____

2. Vs. 5-6. The next morning they had to appear before the _____, _____, _____, and the high _____.

3. Vs. 14-18. Did they have any charges or evidence against the apostles? _____ So what was done? _____

ACTS 5

A similar event happened later. It is described in vs. 17-42.

1. Vs. 17 Who became jealous? _____

2. Vs. 18 What did they do? _____

3. Vs. 19-21 What happened? _____

4. When the apostles were brought before the council they were strictly ordered NOT to _____ (vs. 28). In vs. 29 what was the apostles' reply? _____

5. Vs. 33 and 40. How did the council respond? _____ _____

6. Vs. 41 and 42. Did the apostles give in to the council? _____ What did they do? _____

ACTS 6 Read vs 8-15.
1. A new disciple is described. Who? _____
2. What was he like? _____
3. The old Jews tried to argue Stephen down. Were they successful? (vs. 10) _____
4. So what did they do? _____

ACTS 7
This chapter contains the lengthy address Stephen gave before the council. He reminded them of God's plan for the Jewish nation and how they had continually rejected God's plans and prophets. Now they had rejected and murdered Jesus the Savior.

1. Vs. 54-60 Tell how these people reacted to Stephen's preaching:

_____

_____

2. Tell how Stephen reacted:

_____

_____

This is why Stephen is called the first Christian martyr. A martyr is one who sacrifices his own life for something of great value.

ACTS 8
On the day that Stephen was killed, great persecution began against the church in Jerusalem.

1. Vs. 1 and 3. A new character arises. Who? _____
2. How did he feel about Stephen's death? _____ (Acts 7:58)
3. Was he present at Stephen's stoning? _____
4. How did he treat the early Christians? _____

REMEMBER SAUL. He will be very prominent in future lessons.

UNSCRAMBLE
Those preaching the gospel had been (alejid) _____, (teneab)

_____, (readetneth) _____, and even (likeld) _____.

BUT THEY DID NOT STOP DOING GOD'S WILL!!!!

ACTS 8:4

Those who scattered (from Jerusalem) went about _____ _____

Life for the early Christians was extremely difficult but they continued to do GOD'S will rather than MAN'S. They knew that the Church was a thing of great value because Christ had built the Church and paid for it with His own blood. They were willing to sacrifice to be a part of the Church and become part of God's glorious kingdom. They serve as examples for us today when we encounter difficulties serving God rather than man.

Finish this statement: When the going gets tough, the _____

WHICH CHURCH? (Part 1)

MEMORY VERSE: ACTS 4:12

The church did not begin by accident. It was a result of God's eternal plan. It was foretold in the Old Testament. John the Baptist preached about it and Jesus himself promised to build it.

In many parables Jesus told us of the church's importance and he even sacrificed his own life to establish HIS CHURCH. Much of the New Testament is devoted to teaching about:

- the coming of the church
- the preaching of the gospel
- the establishment of the church
- how to become a member of the church
- how to remain a Christian and a member of Christ's eternal Kingdom.

<u>IT SHOULD BE OBVIOUS THAT GOD INTENDED FOR US TO PLACE EMPHASIS ON THE CHURCH.</u>

The Bible describes the church and what goes on in the church so we can know what a true Christ-established church is like.

What is the Church like?

1. Matthew 16:19 We have already learned that the Church is also called the

    _____

2. Revelation 17:14 Jesus is the King of _____.

3. Matthew 28:18 Jesus has all _____.

4. Colossians 1:13 God has _____ us from darkness and

    _____ us into His Kingdom, where we have

    _____ the Savior.

5. Christians are subjects of Christ's Kingdom and He is our King. This explains Christ's importance to the Kingdom. How many kings does a kingdom have? _____.

6. Colossians 1:18 The church is also described as the _____ and

    Jesus is the _____ of the body.

7. Read 1 Corinthians 12:12-27. What does this teach us about the members of

the "body"? _____

_____

8.   How many heads does a body have? _____

9.   How many bodies does a head have? _____

Since we are parts of the same body that Christ is the head of, we should honor the body and shun all forms of sin and evil which would defile (hurt or damage) the body. God does not want to lose any member of the body, or any member of the body to be hurt or ashamed.

10.   Romans 8:14-17 uses family names to explain our relationship.

    a.   Vs. 14 says we are _____ of God.

    b.   Vs. 16 says we are _____ of God.

    c.   Vs. 17 says we are _____ of God along with Christ.

This shows us that God is like a father who loves and cares for us. A father helps and teaches his children and would not want to lose even one of his children.

What is the Church called?

11.   The church has been called by several names; all would be acceptable to God.

    a. 1 Corinthians 1:2_____

    b. Acts 20:28 _____

    c. 1 Corinthians 12:27 _____

    d. Romans 16:16 _____

What are the Church members called?

12.   In Acts 11:26 we found that the church members were called

_____. They may also be called:

    a. Acts 6:1 _____

    b. Acts 9:13_____

    c. Acts 9:30 _____

    d. Acts 5:14 _____

How do Christians worship?

13.   Acts 20:7 When did the early Christians come together? _____

_____

14. For what purpose? _____

15. Two passages tell other things Christians do in worship. List some of the
things we are to do.

    a. Ephesians 5:19-20 _____

        _____ _____

    b. Colossians 3:16-17 _____

        _____ _____

WHICH CHURCH? (Part 2)

Does it really matter?

Does it really matter what our church members or church or church head is called? Let's see what the Bible says.

1. Acts 4:12 Whose name can we be saved by? _____ Can we be saved by any other name? _____

2. Acts 16:31 Whose name are we to believe in? _____ Do you think another name would do? _____

3. Could we change the church name if we still believed the same things? _____

4. What if an Angel came and told us to change the church? Copy Galatians 1:8 _____

   _____

5. In the Old Testament, what does Deuteronomy 4:2 say about making changes to God's word? _____

   _____

Again, it should be obvious that God has established the nature and "rules" for the church and that it does make a difference if we try to change things. We are to be obedient to God's word and not give in to the will of men or even angels.

6. Proverbs 14:12 tells us that there are ways that seem right to men, but those ways can lead to _____.

7. Matthew 15:9 says that if we believe the doctrine of men that our worship is in _____. This means that it is worthless.

How do you become a Christian?

Look up the references and unscramble the necessary words.

1. _____ Romans 10:14 tells us that we must (reah) first

2. _____ Romans 10:14 also says to (lievbee)

3. _____ Acts 17:30 God said that ever man should

(trepen).

4. _____ Romans 10:10 After the first 3 steps, we must

also (sefnocs) with our mouths.

5. _____ Mark 16:16 Then we must also be (tapzibed).

Once a person has obeyed these steps, he should live a life of service to the Lord Jesus Christ who died for us and made a life in Heaven possible for every one of us. Many passages of scripture in the Bible tell us how a Christian should behave and what characteristics we should have. 2 Corinthians 5:17 tells us that our old sinful person is gone and new things have come. What does this verse say we have become?

_____

TEST YOUR MEMORY

1. Who does the church belong to? _____ Why?

   _____

2. Another name for the church is

   _____.

3. When the church is referred as a body, who is the head?

   _____

4. Members of the church would be referred to as

   _____

5. Can you think of two Biblical names for the church?

   a. _____

   b. _____

6. Church members are called _____ or

   _____ or _____.

7. What things are done during our worship service that are just like what the early church did? _____, _____,

   _____, _____

8. If we are not serious when we are worshipping God, our worship is in

   v_____. (This means no good).

9. Where in the Bible do we learn about the church? _____

10. In your "Keys to Salvation," there are 5 keys that tell you what to do to become a Christian. Can you remember what they are? H_____

    B_____ R_____ C_____, and be

    B_____. There is one other key that is just as important as all of the others. Can you remember which one it is? It is Key #7 _____.

Name _____

Do you think you did well on this Memory Test? _____

PAUL
A CONVERT TO CHRIST
A GREAT TEACHER & PREACHER

MEMORY VERSE: ACTS 19:18

A few weeks ago we first learned about a man called Saul. Saul was a Pharisee and a strict Jew according to their law. That's why Saul was concerned over these disciples of Jesus and their teachings.

1. Acts 9:1-2 tells us what Saul was doing to these disciples. He _____ them and asked for _____ to take to _____ to _____ them and bring them back to _____ for trial and perhaps death.

2. Acts 9:3-9. Read about what happened to Saul as he traveled to Damascus. Make notes so you can discuss this incident in class. _____

   _____

   _____

God had plans for Saul. Read Acts 9:17-21.

1. Who was sent to see Saul? _____ (vs. 17)

2. What happened?

   _____

   _____ (vs. 17-18)

3. He spent time with the _____ in Damascus (vs. 19).

4. He preached _____ as the _____ of _____ (vs. 20).

5. Acts 9:26. When Saul tried to join in with the disciples at Jerusalem they were _____ of him. Why? _____

   _____

6. Acts 9:27. Someone stood up for Saul and explained how he had changed after the incident on the road to _____. Who was it?

_____

7. Acts 13:9. Now Saul will be called _____. This is the name so familiar to all of us.

When Jesus was on earth he picked 12 special men to help him. They were called apostles. Name them

_____ _____ _____ _____

_____ _____ _____ _____

_____ _____ _____ _____

One of these men betrayed Jesus. It was _____, and then there were 11. But someone took his place. It was _____ (Acts 1:23-26) and again there were 12.

Now we read about another disciple called _____. We will find through further study that he came to be one of the greatest teachers and workers for Jesus. He taught about Jesus just as fervently as he had persecuted Christians before the change in his life. Paul was converted to Christ.

Paul traveled many miles, visited many places, endured many hardships all because of his belief in Jesus as God's son.

Paul wrote letters (epistles) to Christians and we will be studying these letters as we continue our study of the New Testament.

1. The New Testament contains _____ books. The first book is _____ and the last is _____.

2. How many books in the Old Testament? _____ which makes a total of _____ in the whole Bible.

Letters to People, Churches, Places

Romans
I Corinthians
II Corinthians
Galations
Ephesians
Philippians
Colossians
I Thessalonians
II Thessalonians
I Timothy
II Timothy
Titus
Philemon
Hebrews
James
I Peter
II Peter
I John
II John
III John
Jude

ROMANS
A LETTER FROM PAUL
MEMORY VERSE: ROMANS 3:23

Last week we learned of Paul's conversion from a hard-lined Mosaic-law Pharisee, to a Christ-like person, a Christian. Many people had problems trusting Paul until they saw his genuine love and sincerity for Christ.

How the church began in Rome is unknown; perhaps by someone who was converted by Peter's preaching on the Day of Pentecost or maybe by Christians from other regions who settled in Rome. Paul had not been to Rome when he wrote this letter. Paul wrote 13 letters (epistles). They are not necessarily in order in the New Testament as they were written. Paul made three journeys to areas and churches to teach, admonish, and encourage Christians. His journeys are called missionary journeys.

Paul wrote the letter to the Romans while he was in Corinth on his third missionary journey. When Paul wrote this letter about three years before going to Rome, he had no idea when he finally did get to Rome it would be as a prisoner.

1. Locate Rome on a map. What country is it in? _____ This

    country is shaped like a _____ and is a part of the continent of

    _____.

CHAPTER 1

1. Paul calls himself a _____ and an apostle of Jesus Christ.

    (Vs. 1)

2. Vs. 9-11. Paul wrote that he _____ for them and

    _____ to visit them soon.

3. Paul in vs. 15-16 says he's ready to come preach the gospel in _____

    because he is not _____ of the _____ of

    _____ for it is the _____

    _____ (finish the sentence).

Paul is writing to a church that is made up of both Jews and Gentiles, but probably more Gentiles. REMEMBER — the gospel of salvation was first preached to the Jews but when they would not accept it, was also given to the Gentiles.

CHAPTER 3

4. Vs. 9-10. Paul says both _____ and _____
    have sinned. There is _____ righteous, _____ not _____.

5. Write the memory verse. _____

    _____

    _____

    Discussion for class: Old-law forgiveness vs. Christ-law forgiveness.

CHAPTER 6

6. Vs. 1. Some might say to Paul, "If Christ through his grace forgives our sins
    then why don't we just keep on sinning so Christ can continue His grace to-
    ward us?" Vs. 2. Paul says, "God _____". In vs. 23 Paul says the
    _____ of sin is _____ but God's gift is _____.

CHAPTER 7

7. Read vs. 15-19. (Read the New English or Modern translation if you have it,
    or have your parents read and discuss the King James version). What is Paul
    saying about himself? _____

    _____

CHAPTER 8

8. Vs. 16-18. The _____ bears witness that we are _____ of
    God. And also _____ even as Christ. If we suffer or have hard-
    ships as Christians, it will not compare to the _____ we
    shall receive in Heaven.

READ: Romans 8:38-39 for class discussion.

_____

_____

CHAPTER 15 (Read Vs. 20-28)

9. Paul says he wanted to come to Rome but has been busy _____
    the gospel in many places. (Vs. 20, 22)

10. Now he is on his way to _____ to take a certain

_____ for the _____ saints. The gift is from the

churches at _____ and _____. (Vs. 25, 26)

11. After finishing this task he plans to be off to _____ but will stop by to see them. (Vs. 24)

CHAPTER 16

12. Phoebe, a good friend of Paul will visit them soon. By the name Paul calls her we know she is a _____ and a _____. ("sister") (Vs. 1)

13. Paul's reference to the church here is "The _____ of _____ salute you." (Vs. 16) Is this a Biblical church name? _____ How do you know? _____

_____

Some points Paul made in his letter to the Roman Christians:

1. To understand about grace and works. Romans 11:6, which is more important? _____

2. Romans 10:17, _____ cometh by _____ and hearing by the _____ of God. We must study and attend Bible classes.

3. Romans 10:9, if we _____ Jesus and believe on Him, we will be _____

4. Romans 12. Vs. 10 _____ one another: (vs. 14) even love and bless those who _____ you.

5. Romans 13:1, 4. _____ the laws of the land. God has given the government authority.

6. Romans 14:10, 12 Don't _____ your brother. Each of us shall give an _____ of himself to _____

7.   ROMANS is the _____ book of the New Testament, its author is

_____

85

I CORINTHIANS
PAUL WRITES A LETTER TO THE CORINTHIANS
MEMORY VERSE: 1 Corinthians 13:13

In Acts 18, we read how Paul visited Corinth and the church began as he taught, and there were believers. Paul preached and taught here for a year and a half.

As Paul traveled on his third missionary journey, he stayed quite some time in Ephesus. It was here he began to hear things about the church in Corinth that concerned him. This letter, 1 Corinthians, was written to the Corinthian Christians from Ephesus.

CHAPTER 1

1. Vs. 1. Paul identifies himself as an _____ of _____

2. Vs. 3. Part of his greeting is that _____ and _____

   from God might be theirs.

   <u>We will learn of some of the problems that existed at Corinth that Paul was concerned about.</u>

Divisions or factions in the church.

3. Vs. 10. In this verse Paul begs them to be of one mind and judgment by (a)

   speaking the _____ and (b) having no

   _____.

4. Vs. 11, 12. Paul said the above about being one or united in their belief because he had heard they claimed to be following _____,

   _____, _____ or _____.

5. Vs. 13. Paul asked "Is Christ _____?" He is teaching that

   while he, Apollos, and Cephas taught them, they were all teaching Christ.

   Therefore, they should all be followers of _____.

CHAPTER 5 – Discipline in the church.

6. Vs. 2. What were they to do about sin? _____

   _____

7. Vs. 7 says to _____ out the old leaven (sin) because

   _____ has made the sacrifice for us.

8. Can sin enter Heaven? _____Should sin be tolerated in the church (kingdom)? _____

CHAPTER 6
9. Vs. 9. Paul tells them that _____ shall not inherit the _____ of _____.

CHAPTER 7 – Marriage vows were not being kept.
10. Vs. 10-11. Paul teaches about marriage. A man and woman, when they marry should stay _____. Let not _____

from the other. In other words, marry for a lifetime.

God does not teach that people should marry, divorce and remarry as they will. He has special teachings concerning divorce and death in a marriage. Every young person should pick their marriage partner considering the kind of person they are and ask, "Do I want this person to be my mate as long as we live?"

CHAPTER 11 – The Lord's Supper. (Some were making the Lord's Supper into a regular meal).
11. Vs. 22. Paul admonishes them to eat at _____ and not shame the

_____ by their behavior.

12. Read vs. 23-29.

    a. Jesus gave the example of the Lord's Supper on the night he was

        _____. (Vs. 23)

    b. The bread represented His _____. (Vs. 24)

    c. The cup represented His _____. (Vs. 25)

    d. When we eat the bread and drink the cup we _____

        Christ's death. (Vs. 26)

    e. Is it important that we do it correctly? _____ What verse do

        you use as proof for your answer? _____

CHAPTER 13 — Importance of love in all things.

This is the greatest chapter on love in the New Testament.

13. This is a wonderful chapter on love. Starting at vs. 4 there is a list of characteristics of love. Name six of them.

   a. _____

   b. _____

   c. _____

   d. _____

   e. _____

   f. _____

CHAPTER 15 – Some were doubting Christs resurrection.

14. Vs. 3-6. First, Paul says Christ _____ was _____ and _____ again. Then, he says it truly happened because he was seen by _____, the _____ and then by _____ brethren at once.

CHAPTER 16 - Teaching on giving.

15. Vs. 1-2. Upon what day were they to give their money? _____ _____ This was a convenient time because they were already together for worship.

16. Since giving is a commandment, is it a part of worship? _____ These collections were to be taken to needy brethren.

17. Paul's letter taught and admonished, but he always expressed his _____ for them. (Vs. 24)

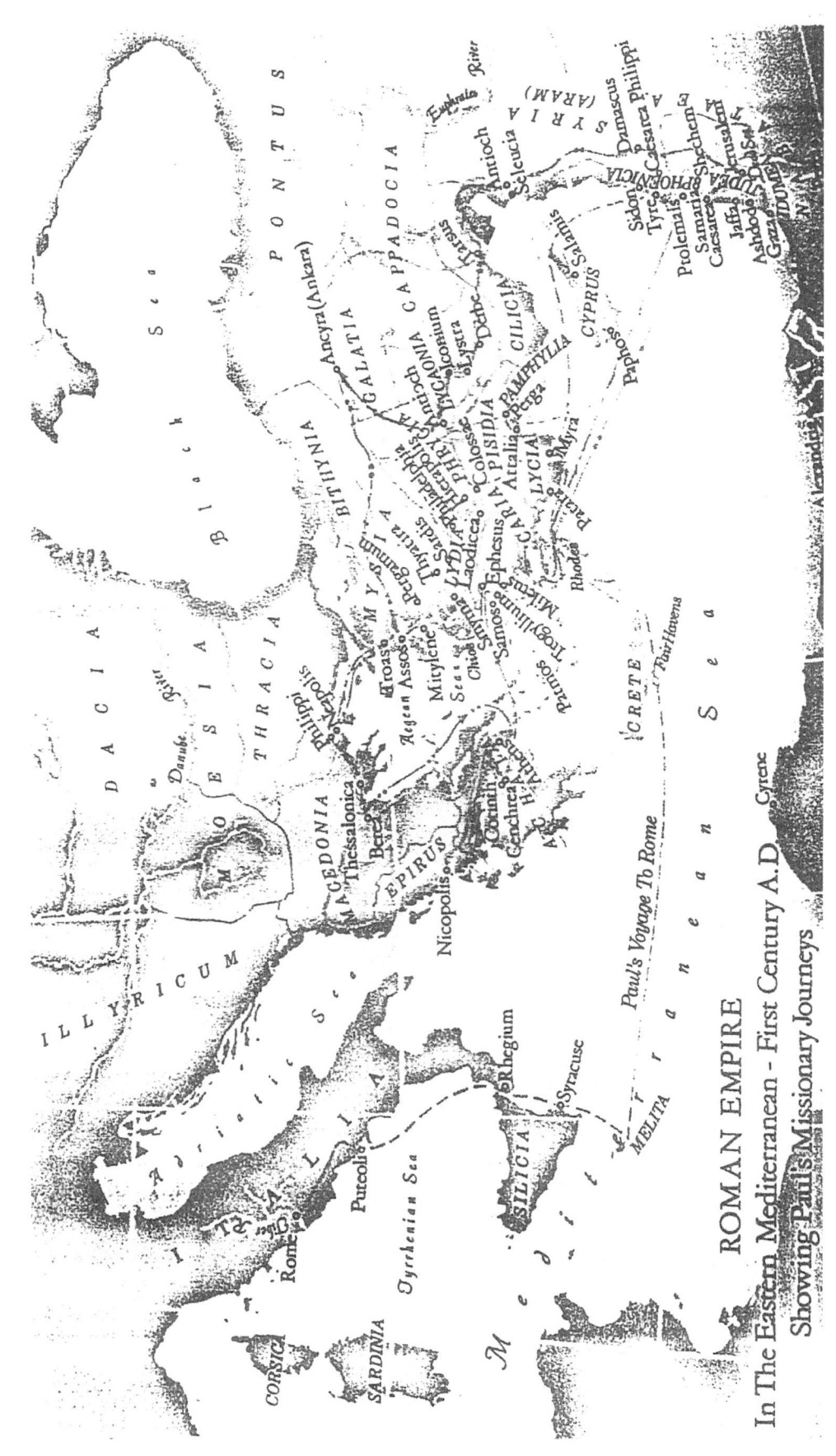

ROMAN EMPIRE
In The Eastern Mediterranean - First Century A.D.
Showing Paul's Missionary Journeys

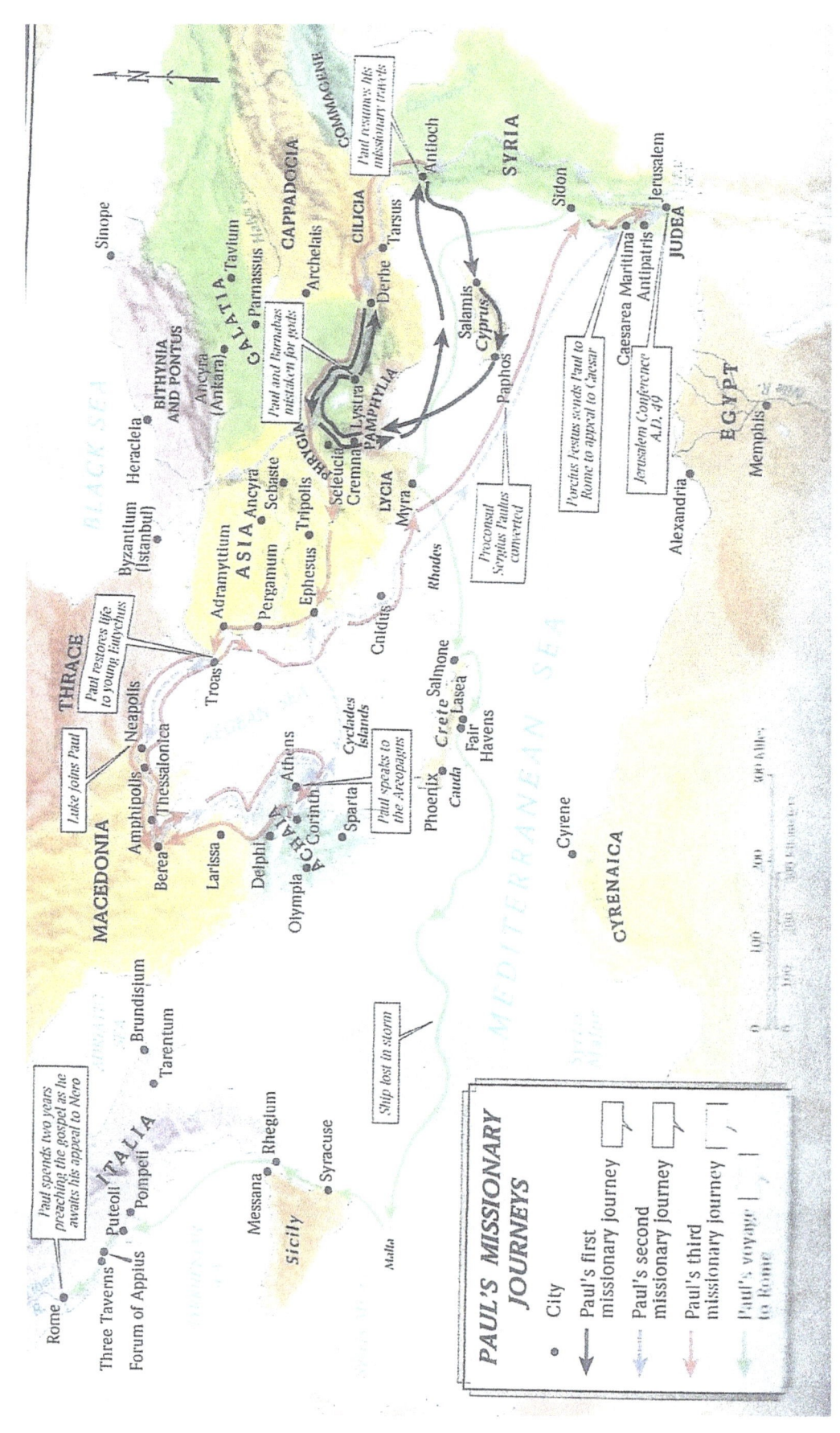

PAUL'S MISSIONARY JOURNEYS

- City
- → Paul's first missionary journey
- → Paul's second missionary journey
- → Paul's third missionary journey
- → Paul's voyage to Rome

Paul spends two years preaching the gospel as he awaits his appeal to Nero

Luke joins Paul

Paul restores life to young Eutychus

Paul speaks to the Areopagus

Ship lost in storm

Paul and Barnabas mistaken for gods

Paul resumes his missionary travels

Proconsul Sergius Paulus converted

Porcius Festus sends Paul to Rome to appeal to Caesar

Jerusalem Conference A.D. 49

2 CORINTHIANS
PAUL'S SECOND LETTER TO THE CORINTHIANS

MEMORY VERSE: 2 Corinthians 5:7

After Paul wrote his first letter to the Corinthians from Ephesus, he was concerned how they would receive his admonishing and teachings. He had been pretty direct in pointing out their problems and wanting them to do what was right. As Paul traveled to Macedonia, Titus, a Christian man, returning from Corinth, told him his letter was received with joy. They had read the letter and corrected some of the problems they were having.

Paul was encouraged and happy to hear this and writes his second letter. in which he continues his teaching.

CHAPTER 1 – Greeting

1. In vs. 1 Paul declares again that he is an

_____ of _____

2. Vs. 2. He wishes for _____ and

_____ to be with them as he did in his first letter.

CHAPTER 2 – Forgiveness

3. Vs. 6-7. After punishment for wrong doing, if a man is sorry for his sin after it was pointed out, we should then be

_____ and comfort him.

4. Vs. 8. We need also to show our _____ for him, lest (vs.

11) _____ might take advantage of him.

CHAPTER 9 – Giving — (Paul again teaches them about giving as he did in his first letter).

5. Read Vs. 6-7. What does vs. 6 mean? _____

_____

Vs. 7 says God loves us if we give _____. How

good is our giving if we give grudgingly? _____

Think about your giving. Do you have an allowance? Do you give anything to the Lord? How do you feel about giving?

6. In giving, Paul points out more than the money part of giving. Read Chpt. 8,

vs. 5 — it tells us to give of _____.

CHAPTER 12 – Paul's Authority and Apostleship

7.   Vs. 12. Paul declares his apostleship was proven among them by _____,

           _____, and _____.

CHAPTER 11

8.   Paul suffered many things because of his preaching of Christ as told in vs. 24-27. Name some of them:

     a.   _____

     b.   _____

     c.   _____

     d.   _____

     e.   _____

     f.   _____

     g.   _____

CHAPTER 13 – Paul Closes His Letter

9.   In vs. 11 Paul says farewell by instructing them to be _____,

     be of _____ ; _____ in peace,

     and God's love and peace would be with them.

10.   Vs. 12. How should they greet each other? _____

     (This was the custom of the day—probably on the cheek).

11.   Read vs. 14. Paul ends his letter with a blessing for them.

     _____

GALATIANS
PAUL WRITES TO CHURCHES IN AN AREA

MEMORY VERSE: Galatians 6:10

This letter from Paul was written to several churches in an area. He had visited this area of Galatia more than once while on his missionary journeys. Some cities in the area were: Antioch, Iconium, Lystra, and Derbe. Paul and Barnabas had visited, taught them, and helped new congregations get started. Once, Paul got sick and was cared for in this area.

Paul's letter was to be read at one congregation then passed on to another until all in the area had read it.

During Paul's absence from them, some Jewish teachers had convinced them that they must also obey some of the old Jewish laws to be Christians. Under Christ, the old law was no longer in effect—it was done away with by Christ's death on the cross.

CHAPTER 1

1. Paul states in vs. 6 that he was surprised or _____ that they were so soon _____ from the gospel.

2. In vs. 8 he says no one can change the gospel, not _____ or an _____. If anyone tries to make changes, they would be _____ (or ruined).

3. Paul reminds them of his conversion from a Jew who persecuted Christians to becoming an apostle for Christ. In vs. 15-16 he states he was called by _____ to _____.

CHAPTER 2

4. Paul points out in vs. 16 that a man is not _____ by works of the old law, but by _____ in _____.

CHAPTER 3

5. In vs. 1 Paul says "O foolish _____ who has _____ or tricked you, that you should not _____ the truth." (They had been misled away from the gospel's teachings).

6. Vs. 13. _____ has redeemed them from the curse of the

_____.

7. Read vs. 24-27. Paul says the law was their _____

    to bring them to _____. After faith in Christ had come,

    they were no longer under the _____ but were children

    of _____ because they were _____ into Christ.

CHAPTER 5

8. Vs. 1. Paul tells them to _____ in their liberty from

    Christ.

9. Vs. 6 tells them that circumcision or uncircumcision is not important in

    Christ, but _____ worketh _____.

10. Paul names some works of the flesh (evil, sin) in vs. 19-21. List some of

    them. _____ _____ _____

    _____ _____ _____

    _____ _____ _____

11. He also names some fruits of the spirit (goodness) in vs. 22-23. Name some

    of them. _____ _____ _____

    _____ _____ _____

    _____ _____ _____

CHAPTER 6

12. Paul says we should care about and for each other. Vs 2 & 9 tells us two
    helpful things we can do as Christians.

    a. _____

    b. _____

13. In vs. 7, Paul says if we sow good we will reap _____ but

    if we sow _____ we will reap _____.

    In other words, if we plant petunias, what will grow? _____

    Paul writes in this letter for those Galatian Christians to stand fast in their faith
in Jesus Christ. Don't listen to those Jewish leaders or anyone who would try to

change the gospel they had been taught.

In today's world, men are still trying to make changes in God's laws to suit themselves. It's God's world and Christ's church and God's laws. Paul's message is still true, "If anyone tries to change God's word, he will be accursed." Galatians 1:9.

EPHESIANS
A LETTER OF INFORMATION AND INSTRUCTION

MEMORY VERSE: Ephesians 2:8

Paul spent about three years in Ephesus, according to Acts 20.

As we study the Acts of the Apostles, we follow Paul's journey from Corinth to Jerusalem. Because he taught about Jesus to the Gentiles, he made enemies among the Jews and was arrested falsely. Also, people of the area of Ephesus were great idol worshippers of the Goddess Diana. Many craftsmen made their living by creating these idols for people to worship. As Paul and his friends taught Christianity, these craftsmen became angry and wanted to get rid of Paul.

Since he was also a Roman citizen, he could demand to have a trial by Caesar (the king). Paul was taken to Rome and held a prisoner for about two years in a rented house.

During his imprisonment in Rome, Paul continued to preach about the Kingdom of God. He wrote several letters to churches or areas while there. Among them is the letter to the Ephesians. Paul's Godly teachings in this letter are not on a specific subject, but are of a general theme. This letter was probably read at the Ephesus church and then passed on to other churches in surrounding areas.

When Paul wrote to them, he taught about unity, how all Christians were one family and should love each other. He writes about the church—not a building, but the people. We learn that a Christian in gentle and longsuffering, kind and peaceful. We learn how to protect ourselves from the devil by putting on the armor of faith.

CHAPTER 1

1. Vs. 5 — Jesus is God's own Son and as we become Christians we become

    God's children also. Paul refers to us as _____ children.

2. Vs. 7 — Paul writes here, "In whom we have _____

    through his blood, the _____ of sin."

    a. Look up "redemption" in the dictionary and write the meaning.

    _____

    _____

    b. Whose blood is Paul referring to? _____

3. Vs. 19-23 — Paul is explaining God's power and the working. He tells these

    Christians at Ephesus something about God's magnificent power.

96

a. His power _____ Jesus from the dead.

b. His power makes Jesus greater than all _____ and

_____ and _____

and _____ and every _____

named in this world and in the world to come. (What world is to

come? _____)

c. God's power made Jesus _____ over all tilings to the

church.

CHAPTER 2

4. Vs. 5-8 — Paul points out how God shows His favor to us (Christians).

a. We were _____ in sin.

b. God _____ us up together, to sit together with

_____ in heavenly places (the Church).

c. To show the exceeding _____ of his _____

and _____ toward us through Jesus.

d. For by _____ are you saved through _____ (trust)

and not of yourselves, it is a _____ of God.

5. Vs. 9-10 — Paul tells them they cannot be saved through their

_____ . The gift of Jesus was so costly it could never be

repaid no matter how much we worked. But, to show our appreciation for

this great gift of Jesus, and because we are God's workmanship, created like

Jesus, we should do _____ .

6. Vs. 13 — Paul points out that the Gentiles, referred to here as those who

"sometimes were far off,' are brought near by the _____ of

Christ.

a. Vs. 14 — The wall of _____ between Jews and

Gentiles has been broken down.

b. Vs. 16 — Reconciled to God by the _____.

c. Vs. 17 — Through His preaching to them of _____.

d. Vs. 19 — They become _____-_____, no more strangers and foreigners in God's house.

CHAPTER 4

7. Paul talks to these Christians in Ephesus about walking in unity. With _____ and _____, with _____ in love, we keep the _____ of the Spirit in _____. (Vs. 2-3)

   a. Vs. 4-6 — How many "ones" do you find? _____ Write them. _____

_____

   b. If unity is so important to God, does he approve or want all of these different churches? _____ How many churches did Jesus die for? _____

8. Read verses 14-16 for discussion in class.

9. Vs. 24-31 — Paul talks about the new person, the Christian. He lists some "do nots." Name four of them:

   a. _____

   b. _____

   c. _____

   d. _____

10. Some "do's" in vs. 32 are: be _____ one to another, tenderhearted, _____ one another even as God for _____ sake forgives you.

CHAPTER 5 & 6

11. Families are important to God. Paul writes some instructions for members of a family.

a. Chpt. 5:25 — _____, love your wives even as Christ loved the church.

b. Chpt. 5:33 — A wife must _____ her husband.

c. Chpt. 6:1 — _____, obey your parents in the Lord for this is _____.

12. Chpt. 6:13-17 — Paul talks about armor that will protect a Christian. He tells us to wear this armor.

a. Loins girded with _____.

b. Breastplate of _____.

c. Feet shod with _____ of _____.

d. Shield of _____.

e. Helmet of _____.

f. Sword of the _____.

Satan will not bother the strong, if we are weak he will be able to get into our lives and influence us. If we wear our Christian armor, Satan can not defeat us.

This letter from Paul can influence our lives today even as in the long ago at Ephesus.

PHILIPPIANS
PAUL'S LETTER TO A CHURCH IN MACEDONIA

MEMORY VERSE: Philippians 4:4

Philippi is located in the country of Macedonia. Paul was across the sea in the Galatian area on his second missionary journey, when he had a vision in the night. In this vision, a man appeared and begged him to come over to Macedonia and preach there. Paul knew God was directing him where he should go and preach. This is the first preaching of the gospel in Europe.

They arrived at this great military city of Philippi, and on the Sabbath day (Saturday) went where the people were gathered down by the river (there was no synagogue here).

Paul preached about Jesus, and it was here he met Lydia, a religious woman, and one we learn was a good and kind and helpful woman to her household and neighbors. She was a seller of purple, or a business woman who wove fabrics and dyed them in purples, which was in great demand at that time.

It was here in Philippi also that Paul cast devils from a girl. Her masters were very angry because they had used this girl to tell fortunes and make money. Paul, along with Silas, was beaten and cast into prison; and while they were there, they sang and prayed. At midnight an earthquake came and the jail doors were opened and their chains fell off. The jailer, having heard Paul and Silas and their praise to God, believed and was baptized, along with all his household.

When do you think they were saved: when they believed? Or when they were baptized?

So, through a woman, a girl, and a man, the church began in Philippi. Later, while Paul was imprisoned in Rome, Italy, he wrote this letter to the Philippian church.

Chapter 1

1. Paul says in vs. 1 that this letter comes from him and also from

    _____.

2. Paul prays for these Christians. Vs. 9 — he prays that their

    _____ may abound. Vs. 11 — and that they might be filled

    with fruits of _____.

3. Paul makes a statement that may sound strange to you. In vs. 23 and 24, he

    says he is torn between two things; whether to _____ and

    be with _____ or to _____ in the flesh,

which was needful to them. (We'll discuss this further in class).

CHAPTER 2

4. Paul teaches on unity and humility in vs. 2-5.

    a. Be _____ having the same love.

    b. Be of _____ mind.

    c. Let nothing be done through _____

    d. Think of others ahead of _____

    e. Let your mind be like _____

5. Read vs. 8. Who is Paul talking about here?

    _____

6. Paul tells them of the holiness and greatness of Jesus in vs. 10 and 11. He says at the name of Jesus every _____ should bow and every _____ should confess.

7. Special instructions from Paul in vs. 14. Write it down.

    _____

CHAPTER 3

8. Paul uses his life as a teaching:

    a. First, in vs. 6, he says with _____ he _____ the church.

    b. After learning of Christ, in vs. 8 he says, "I have suffered the _____ of all things that I may win _____."

    c. And, in vs. 14, he presses toward the _____ of the high calling of God in _____.

CHAPTER 4

9. In vs. 8, Paul as he closes his letter to these Christians, points out some things to consider. "Finally brethren, whatsoever things are _____, are _____, are _____,

are _____, are lovely, are of

_____, think on these things."

10. Paul tells them in vs. 9, "these things which ye have both learned and seen in

me, _____, and God's _____ shall be with you."

11. Earlier in this letter Paul says he lost or gave up all for Christ. In vs, 11, he

says "I have learned in whatsoever _____ I am, therewith to be

_____."

Paul wrote this letter from Rome while a prisoner there. In this letter he points out the importance of unity, humility (avoiding strife), and obedience.

Paul used his life as an example to point out that although we may have had hardships along the way, Heaven will be worth it all! Just as Paul was helped by these Christians when he had needs; we know our fellow Christians are there to help and encourage us. Where else do we find such caring people as in the Church?

COLOSSIANS
PAUL WRITES A PASS-AROUND LETTER

MEMORY VERSE: See below #11

This letter by Paul was written while a prisoner in Rome, the same as the letters to the Ephesians and Philippians. It was written to a church where Paul had never been. However, he had heard of this church from his close friend Epaphras.

The spiritual life of this church was being threatened by some misguided teachers. Paul wrote this letter to correct these false teachings and to point out the supreme headship of Christ, who was above all others.

CHAPTER 1

1. A minister had visited them and taught them, who was he? (Vs. 7)

   _____

2. Vs. 12-14. Paul writes of his thanks to _____ who had delivered us from _____ into the kingdom of his dear _____. In _____ we have _____ through his _____, the _____ of sin (This applies to Paul, those Colossians, and even to us today).

CHAPTER 2

3. Paul warns them about false teachers.

   a. Vs. 16. Let no man judge you on _____ or _____ or special _____ days.

   b. Vs. 18. Let no man rob you of _____ and have you worship _____.

   c. Vs. 8. Beware of men of _____ deceit, who would have you follow the traditions of _____ and not after _____

4. Paul reminds them of their commitment to Christ.

    a. Vs. 6. As you have therefore received _____

       the Lord, so _____ you in him.

    b. Vs. 7. _____ and built up in him, established in the

       faith as ye have been _____.

CHAPTER 3

5. Vs. 2. Set your _____ on things above and not on
_____ of the _____. (Good thoughts for
us—what things are important in your life?)

6. Paul advises them to remove some sinful things in their life and add some
good things.

    a. Vs. 8 Remove: _____, _____,
_____, _____, and
_____.

    b. Vs. 12 Add: _____, _____,
_____, _____ and above all,
put on _____ (love) Vs. 14.

7. Paul says in vs. 17, whatever we do in word or deed, we should do all in the
_____ of the Lord, _____.

CHAPTER 4

8. Read vs. 1. Let's discuss in class.

9. Paul tells them to be examples to those outside the church by...

    a. Walking in _____(Vs. 5) (discussion)

    b. Let your speech be with _____(Vs. 6) (discussion)

10. Vs. 16. This letter was written to Colossae, but Paul tells them to exchange
and share letters with the _____.

11. Above all, Paul tells them in Chapter 3:16, Let the _____ of Christ
dwell in you richly in all _____, teaching and admonishing one
_____in _____ and _____ and
_____ songs, singing with _____ in your
_____ to the Lord.

I THESSALONIANS
A LETTER ABOUT JESUS' SECOND COMING
MEMORY VERSE: Name the 12 Apostles

Recite the books of the New Testament to where we are now.

On his second missionary journey, Paul stopped by Thessalonica with Silas. As usual, he found the synagogue and began to preach. Many who listened were converted to Christ. But there were some Jewish leaders who were jealous. These men caused a riot, and the house where Paul stayed was attacked. Some Christians were arrested and charged with treason because they claimed another king, Jesus instead of Caesar. They were finally released. We read of this in Acts 17:1-9.

Paul and Silas fled the city to another place but Paul was concerned about the Christians at Thessalonica. While at Corinth Paul heard from Timothy about them. They were standing fast in spite of sufferings. From Corinth he wrote this letter to encourage them, to confirm their faith and give them additional teachings on Christ's second coming. (Do you know and understand about Christ's second coming? We will have some discussion about this in our class period).

CHAPTER 1

1. After Paul's usual greeting when he writes a letter to a church, he comments on their faith and belief. In vs. 7 he says "they were _____ to all."

2. In vs. 8 he says "the _____ of the Lord was spread in _____ and _____ and surrounding areas because of their great faith.

CHAPTER 2

3. In this chapter Paul writes how they came to teach them of Christ even though it brought wrath from the unbelievers.

    a. Vs. 11. Paul says he _____ and _____ and _____ them as a father does his children.

    b. Vs. 12. The reason for doing this exhorting and teaching was to have them walk _____ of God who has called them to His _____ (the church).

CHAPTER 3

4. Since Paul could not go, he sent someone back to Thessalonica to check on the brethren there. In vs. 2, who was sent?

_____

5. Vs. 6. Did Timothy come back with a good report? _____

6. Paul commended them on their _____ and

_____.

CHAPTER 4

7. Vs. 9, 11, 12. Paul mentions several important things their lives as Christians should contain:

a. Love each other, _____ love.

b. Study to be _____, not busy bodies but minding their own business.

c. Walk _____, uprightly, so that others may see your example.

8. Vs. 13-17, here Paul talks about the second coming of Christ.

a. Christ shall _____ from heaven with a _____ from the _____. (vs. 16)

b. Those who have died will _____ bring with him. (vs. 14)

c. Those still living will be _____ up in the _____ with the Lord. (vs. 17)

CHAPTER 5

9. Paul continues his writing about Jesus second coming. In vs. 1-2 he says they don't need to know when that day will be. It will come as a

_____ in the night. (Does a thief advertise when he will strike?)

10. Vs. 6. Paul is saying "be on guard," be _____ of Jesus coming.

11. Vs. 14. Paul tells them to be helpful to others:

    a. _____ the unruly (disobedient)

    b. _____ the feebleminded (fainthearted)

    c. _____ the weak

    d. _____ toward all men.

12. Read verse 21 carefully for class discussion.

II THESSALONIANS
A LETTER OF ENCOURAGEMENT AND TEACHING

MEMORY WORK: (1) This letter has 3 chapters. (2)This book is a letter written by Paul (3) This letter is written from Corinth

Paul, Silas, and Timothy are still at Corinth when this second letter was written to the church at Thessalonica. Only a short time had passed since Paul had written the first letter (I Thessalonians), but it seems someone had written another letter and pretended it was from Paul. (Chpt. 2:2)

Christians at this church are suffering some persecutions and some have stopped working, thinking Jesus was coming now!

CHAPTER 1

1. Vs. 3. Paul thanks God for the Christians in this church because their faith

   _____ and their love _____.

CHAPTER 2

2. Vs. 3. Paul tells them not to be _____ by anyone.

   The _____ when Jesus comes again will not come un-

   til certain things take place.

3. Vs. 3-4. An evil person will come and _____ himself as

   a God.

4. What will God finally do to this person? (Vs. 8)

   _____ him with the breath of his

   _____.

5. Vs. 15. Christians are to stand _____ and _____

   the traditions which they were _____.

6. Vs. 12. Those who do not believe will be _____.

CHAPTER 3

7. God does not like idleness. In Vs. 10 he says if anyone

   _____ work, neither shall he _____.

8. Read Vs. 11-12. We'll discuss these verses in class.

9.   Vs. 13. Paul says "do not grow _____ in doing good."

Throughout this short letter, the promise of God's victory over evil is stressed. Christians may suffer now, but God's planned reward will be worth it all! For those who refuse to obey God, there will be distress and judgment.

Did you know you honor God with a good life, and shame Him when you are bad?

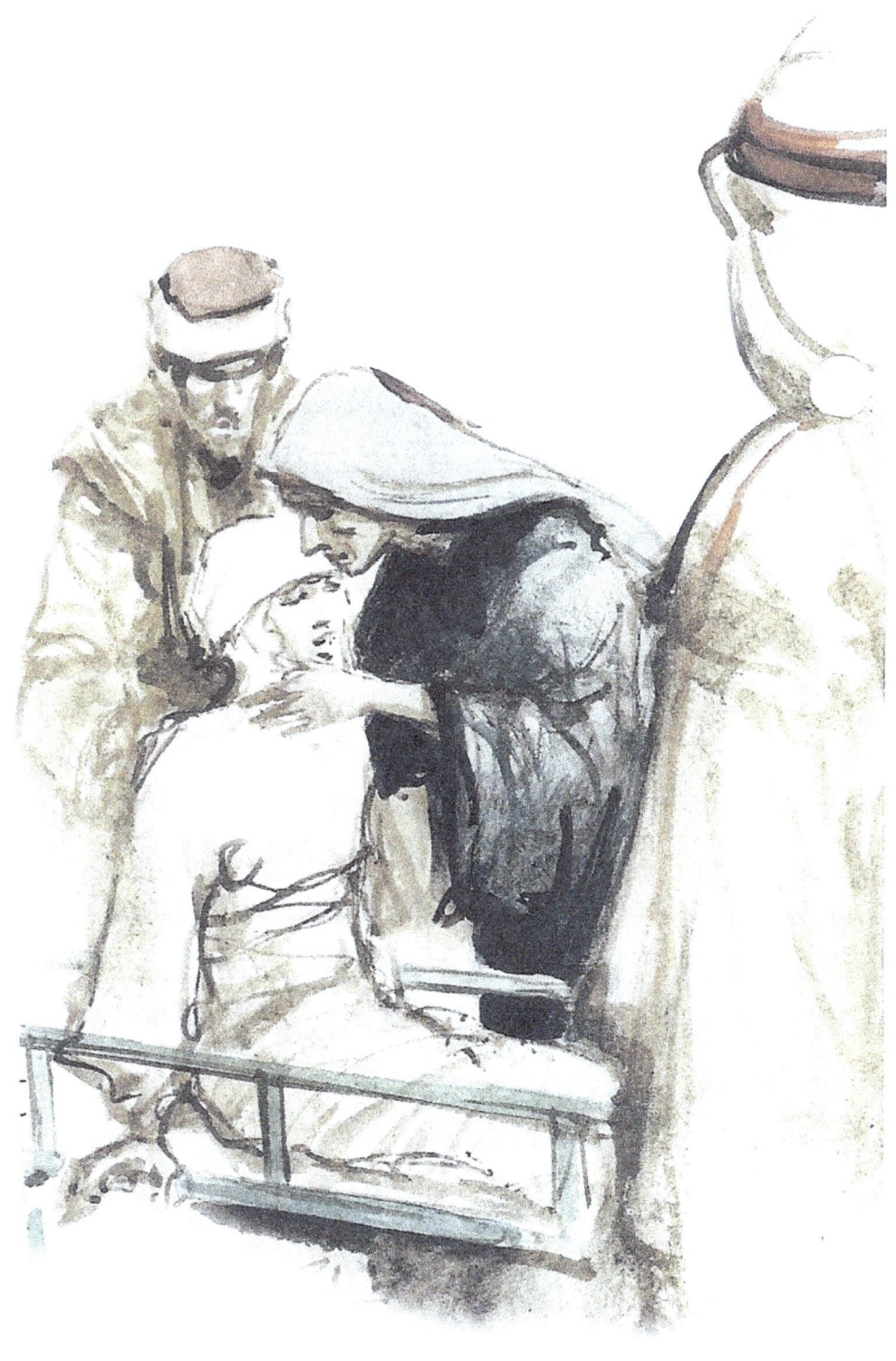

OUR WORSHIP TO GOD

1. What is worship? _____

   _____

   _____

2. When did the early Christians meet? 1 Corinthians 16:2 _____

   _____

ACTS OF WORSHIP -PRAYER: (to request with zeal)

1. James 5:16. We are to pray for _____ for

   _____.

2. Matthew 21:22. When we pray we should _____ and we

   will _____.

3. Ephesians 5:20. Give _____ always for all things to

   _____ through _____.

SINGING: (celebrate in song)

1. Ephesians 5:19. _____ and making melody in your

   _____ to the Lord.

2. Read Colossians 3:16. How did they make melody? _____

   These are instructions concerning our worship of singing—is a musical instrument mentioned in these scriptures? _____ Did you know — musical instruments are not mentioned anywhere in the New Testament as a part of the worship of the church.

PREACHING: (speaking publicly on a religious subject)

1. 2 Timothy 2:15. If we study God's word we will have His _____.

   By "rightly dividing" the word (reading and studying it) we will know what

   God expects of us.

2. Romans 10:17. How do we increase our faith? _____

3. 2 Peter 3:18. We give God glory by growing in _____ of His

word.

4.   Acts 2:38. The first sermon of the Church was preached in _____

by _____ on the Day of _____. What

resulted from the preaching of this sermon? _____

_____ vs.41

LORD'S SUPPER: (remembering Jesus' sacrifice for our sins)
1.   Acts 20:7 states the disciples came together when? _____

_____ To do what two things: (a) _____

(b) _____

2.   1 Corinthians 11:29. Is taking the Lord's Supper a serious thing?

_____ Why?

_____

GIVING: (everything belongs to God, it is on loan to us)
1.   2 Corinthians 9:7. Three things about giving are taught: as we

_____; not _____ but

_____.

2.   1 Corinthians 16:2. When did the early Christians give; and since this is an

example for us, when should we give?

_____

From what we have just studied we find our worship to God should be reverent, respectful, joyful, happy, and serious.

If we are honoring God with our worship, circle the following things we should do ... . and put an X by things we should not be doing during worship.

Talking	singing	writing notes
paying attention	sleeping	listening
thinking of words in songs	laughing	using our Bibles
	goofing off	

BIBLE QUIZ

1.   Name the Gospels:

        a. _____

        b. _____

        c. _____

        d. _____

2.   What does "gospel" mean? _____

3.   Name all the apostles whose name begins with "J".

        a. _____

        b. _____

        c. _____

        d. _____

        e. _____

4.   What book of the New Testament tells of the beginning of the Church?

    _____

5.   What books tell of Jesus birth, life and death? _____

6.   What was Jesus first miracle? _____

7.   Tell three things you know about Jesus birth.

        a. _____

        b. _____

        c. _____

8.   What did the man do when his son, who had wasted his inheritance, returned

    home? _____

    _____

9.   Name 3 characteristics of Jesus.

        a. _____

b. _____

c. _____

10. Name the apostles.

a. _____

b. _____

c. _____

d. _____

e. _____

f. _____

g. _____

h. _____

i. _____

j. _____

k. _____

l. _____

m. _____

n. _____

11. One apostle died — who was he? _____

a. Who took his place? _____

12. Who preached the first gospel sermon? _____

13. Peter said he would never leave Jesus, but Jesus said he would deny Him three times before what happened? _____

14. How did the soldiers secure Jesus grave? _____

15. The Church began on what special day? Day of _____.

16. When the apostles preached at the beginning of the Church, there were people from many different areas and many different languages. What unusual thing occurred? _____

17. The Church belongs to Jesus. Why? _____

18. How do we get into the Church? _____

_____

19. On the first day of the Church, how many were saved? _____

20. Tell what you know about Stephen. _____

_____

21. On the road to Damascus a life was changed. Who was it and how did his

life change?

_____

_____

22. What is an epistle? _____ Several of these were

written by Paul. Can you name two? _____

23. There are 5 steps to be taken to be saved. Can you name them?

     a. _____

     b. _____

     c. _____

     d. _____

     e. _____

24. How many churches did Jesus say He would build? _____ He

said "I will build *my* Church." Will any Church do? _____

25. Another name for the Church is _____

26. Name some things that are a part of our worship service. _____

_____

27. Explain the Lord's Supper. _____

_____

    a. When was it given and why? _____

_____

_____

b. How often do we observe this supper?

_____

_____

28. Paul was in prison in Rome. Where is Rome — what country? _____

Shaped like a _____.

29. Paul wrote two letters to the Corinthians. Name the 2 books that are these

letters. _____

30. How many books in the New Testament? _____

31. Tell some things about Jesus death. _____

_____

_____

32. Jesus died, rose from His death to live again and is now in Heaven. What

wonderful thing will happen when He comes again?_____

_____

a. Will Jesus walk on this earth again as He did before? _____

b. Where will we meet Jesus when He comes again? _____

I TIMOTHY
A LETTER TO A BELOVED FRIEND

MEMORY VERSE: 1 Timothy 1:15

All of Paul's letters we have studied so far have been written to individual churches or churches in a certain area. The next three books of the New Testament are letters written to people Paul knew.

Timothy and Paul had a very close relationship. Paul taught and converted Timothy—he was like a son. They had traveled together, taught and worked together.

Timothy lived at Lystra. He had been carefully trained in the old law by his Jewish mother Eunice and his grandmother Lois. His father was a Greek.

Paul's letters to Timothy concerned teachings of church leadership and training of its members to be the church as Christ meant it to be. It is uncertain where Paul was when he wrote this letter, but fairly certain he was no longer a prisoner in Rome.

CHAPTER 1

1. Paul calls Timothy his _____ in verse 2.

2. Timothy is at _____ at this time (Vs. 3)

CHAPTER 2

3. Read verses 1 and 2. Who does Paul tell Timothy we are to pray for? All in

    _____ and _____ that we may live in

    _____. From this teaching we see it is important that we pray

    for leaders of our country, for our president, that the United States of America

    may remain free and peaceful.

4. In verse 8, Paul writes that men should _____ and in verse 9 that

    women should adorn (dress) themselves in

    _____.

5. Read verses 11 and 12. A woman's role in church leadership is pointed out.

    She should be _____ and not have _____

    over men.

CHAPTER 3

In the church we have Elders (Bishops), Deacons, Preachers, and Teachers. This chapter teaches what God expects of two of these leaders.

6. The position of an Elder (Bishop) is so important to the church that in verse 1 Paul writes "a man should _____ the position." Elders look after the souls of men so they need to desire this serious work.

7. Read verses 2-7.

   a. A Bishop (Elder) must have only _____ wife. (vs. 2)

   b. Things he must not be are: (vs. 3)

      1. _____

      2. _____

      3. _____

      4. _____

8. Deacons are to help with the work of the church. They are servants. Read verses 8-13. We will discuss these verses in class. Verse 13 states a Deacon who serves _____ obtains a _____ standing in the faith in Christ Jesus.

CHAPTER 4

9. Verse 12. Timothy is a young man but Paul tells him to be an

   _____ in _____, in _____, in

   _____, in _____, and in _____.

CHAPTER 5

10. In this chapter Paul writes about taking care of widows, respecting older men, honoring Elders and, in verse 21, he tells Timothy to treat all people

    _____.

CHAPTER 6

11. Verse 1. Paul writes to Timothy that servants who become Christians should still _____ their masters.

12. Paul warns in verse 9 that the desire to be _____ can sometimes bring temptations. Verses 7-8 teach we should be content with what _____ and _____ we have.

13. Verse 11. Timothy is to pursue (seek after) _____,

_____, _____,

_____, and _____.

14. Verse 12. Timothy is told by Paul to fight the good fight of faith and _____ on eternal life.

15. In this letter we are taught as Timothy was to guard our lives from sin, fight the good fight of faith and lay hold on eternal life. In Chapter 6:18, Paul directs Christians to be _____ in good works, ready to _____, and willing to _____.

Do you know the Elders and Deacons of your congregation?
- Elders

_____

_____

- Deacons

_____

_____

2 TIMOTHY
PAUL WRITES HIS FINAL LETTER

MEMORY VERSE: 2 Timothy 2:15

Even though we still have the book (epistle) of Titus to study, it is believed that 2 Timothy was the last letter Paul wrote during his lifetime. Paul had been arrested a second time and brought to Rome again as a prisoner. While awaiting death he wrote this letter.

Paul expresses to Timothy that even though his earthly life might end, God has an eternal life waiting for him in heaven.

CHAPTER 1

1. Paul again refers to Timothy as his _____ (vs. 2), and in verse 3, Paul says he _____ night and day for Timothy.

2. In verse 8, Paul says "do not be _____ of the testimony of God," and in verse 13, he tells Timothy to

    _____ to the sound words he has taught him.

CHAPTER 2

3. Vs. 2. Paul tells Timothy to pass on to others the things he has taught him. "Commit to _____ men." They, in turn, would pass on — and on — until it comes down to us. Isn't that wonderful that God's word has been kept alive down through the ages to us? What would have happened to us if this had not been done?

4. What do you think verse 11 means?

    _____

5. Read verses 22 — 24. Paul writes to Timothy of some things we should and some things we should not do. Name a few of each

    Should

    _____

    _____

    _____

119

Should Not

_____

_____

_____

CHAPTER 3

6.   Paul warns of _____ in verse 1. Men will turn away from God's ways. What are some of the dungs men will do? (vs. 2-5)

_____

_____

_____

_____

7.   What might happen to Christians? (vs. 12)

_____

_____

8.   Read vs. 16-17. In these verses we are told that God's word will help us to live as He wants us to, will answer our questions, will help the man of God (Christian) to be _____

CHAPTER 4

9.   Verse 1 & 2. Paul charges (seriously urges) Timothy to _____ the word. Be _____ at all times to teach.

10.   Verse 6 & 7. Paul says his departure (death) is _____. He said, "I have _____ the good _____, _____ the race and kept the _____."

11.   Verse 8. Paul's _____ of righteousness is ready for him;

will be given to him by the

_____ on that _____.

(What does this mean?

_____

_____)

12. Paul hopes Timothy will be able to come and see him before his death. In
verse 9 he says come _____ and in verse 21 he says try to
"come before _____."

Paul is not afraid; he has fought a good fight, finished the race and is ready to
receive his crown (vs. 7 & 8). A more faithful man we will not read about. He has
endured many hardships since his conversion and faithfulness to Christ
   HOPEFULLY, WE WILL NEVER HAVE TO ENDURE PAUL'S HARD-
SHIPS . . . BUT, IF WE SHOULD, COULD WE?

WRITE 5 SENTENCES ABOUT PAUL. WRITE WHATEVER YOU KNOW OR RE-MEMBER THAT WE HAVE STUDIED.

1. _____

_____

2. _____

_____

3. _____

_____

4. _____

_____

5. _____

_____

TITUS

ONE OF PAUL'S ADOPTED SONS

MEMORY VERSE: Titus 2:11

Titus was a Gentile. Remember how Titus brought word from Corinth after Paul wrote his first letter to them (1 Corinthians) and took the second one back (2 Corinthians). Paul's friend and associate Titus had been left on the island of Crete to teach and strengthen the church there. Some of these Jewish Christians were converts from the church's beginning in Jerusalem.

Paul became so attached to these young men that they became like his family. Our church family is sometimes closer to us than our own physical family because we are striving to go to Heaven and we encourage each other.

It is believed that Paul wrote this letter, the next to last one he wrote, from Nicopolis. The last letter he wrote, you will remember, was _____.

CHAPTER 1

1. In verse 4, Paul calls Titus his _____. What other man did Paul call his son? _____

2. Titus is at Crete instructing the new Christians on how God wants them to be. Paul again gives instructions about Elders in the church. In recent lessons we said Elders and _____ were the same. In verse 5-9, Paul list some qualifications. We have already studied some of these but let's discuss again.

    a. Husband of _____ wife.

    b. Have _____ children.

    c. Lover of what is _____.

    d. _____ to the faithful words he has been taught.

3. Next we have the Elders' task or job. In verses 10-12 we read about some troublemakers. In verse 13, Paul tells Titus to _____ them sharply that they might change and be _____ in the faith. All correcting done by an Elder should be done with _____.

CHAPTER 2

4. Verse 1. Paul says speak only _____ doctrine.

5. In verse 2-8 are instructions for different ages of men and women. List something for each one.

   Older men. _____

   Older women. _____

   Young women. _____

   Young men. _____

6. Verse 11. God's grace brings _____ to all men.

7. Verse 12. To gain God's grace we must _____.

8. Verse 15. Paul tells Titus to speak these things with all _____.

CHAPTER 3

9. Remember, we have talked about obeying laws of the land. Verse 1 says we are subject to _____.

10. Verse 2-4. Paul tells Titus to instruct those at Crete to speak _____ of no one, be _____ and _____. Why? Read verse 3. We will discuss in class.

11. Verse 9. Concerning the old law, Paul says to avoid _____ disputes and _____ about the law because it is _____. After all, the old law (Law of Moses) is gone with the cross of _____, and we now live under the new Christian law (Law of Christ).

We have spent several weeks now studying about and learning from the letters written by Paul to churches, to an area of churches, and to individual Christians.

Paul should be an inspiration to all of us—he went from one who persecuted those who would follow Jesus, to a great apostle and teacher of Christ. We should never be ashamed to tell others that we believe in and serve Jesus.

PHILEMON
A PLEA TO A FRIEND

MEMORY VERSE: John 3:16

This is a short letter written by Paul to his friend and fellow Christian, Philemon, who lived at Colossae. Paul wrote from his prison home in Rome.

He wrote this letter specifically to tell Philemon of the conversion of his runaway slave Onesimus. Paul has taught Onesimus and has love for him.

READ the entire chapter before you begin the questions—there is only one chapter in this book. Pay particular attention to the divisions — Greetings, Philemon's Love and Faith, etc.

1. Vs. 1, Paul calls Philemon a _____ friend and

   _____.

2. Vs. 4-7. Paul compliments Philemon on his _____ and

   _____ toward Jesus and the saints. By

   _____ his faith he has shown his goodness in

   _____. The saints at Colos-

   sae have been _____ (encouraged) by Phi-

   lemon and Paul feels great _____ over this.

3. Vs. 8-10. Paul asks a favor of Philemon concerning

   _____.

4. Vs. 12-14. Paul _____ Onesimus back even

   though he wished to _____ him in Rome but could not with-

   out the _____ of Philemon,

5. Vs. 16. Onesimus is still Philemon's slave by law, but now that he is a

   Christian he is also a _____ to Philemon in

   Christ.

6. Vs. 17-19. Paul wants Philemon to forgive Onesimus for running away,

   and any other wrong he has done. He says he (Paul) will _____

   anything owed.

7.   Vs. 21. Paul has confidence that _____ will do what is right.

8.   In what verse do you read where Paul hopes to visit Colossae?

     _____

9.   Paul's farewell is one that he uses often in his letters, "The _____ of our Lord Jesus Christ be with your _____. Amen."

Paul said Onesimus had been helpful to him in Rome and would certainly be helpful to Philemon upon his return, now that it was with a Christian attitude.

This short book (letter) points out how we are changed when we become Christians. Onesimus wanted to do what was right, even though it meant going back to his master. I'm sure Philemon treated him differently too—after all they are Christian brothers now, even though still master and slave. Perhaps, in time, Philemon gave him his freedom

Next week we will have a review of Paul's conversion and life. Hopefully, you will remember many things about Paul's life, but you may want to use your previous lessons or a Bible concordance.

AN APOSTLE CALLED PAUL

This lesson is a review of the life of the great apostle Paul. You can use your lesson sheets or a concordance to help with the answers you do not know.

1. Before being called Paul, he was known as _____

2. Paul was a _____ (nationality) of the _____ sect.

3. Was Paul a religious man? _____

4. In Acts 9, we read of Paul's conversion to Christianity. He was

   _____ on a road to _____. His purpose for the trip

   was to _____ Christians and return them to _____

   to _____ or _____.

5. As Paul traveled along this road a bright light came down and he was

   _____. He heard a voice speak and knew it was the

   _____. Paul's friends led him on to the city where

   _____ came and taught him. Paul was then

   _____ and became a Christian.

6. Paul immediately started preaching. From Jerusalem he made

   _____ missionary journeys.

7. After visiting these different cities and helping to start churches he would

   write them letters (sometimes called _____). Some letters

   he wrote were to the: R_____, P_____,

   T_____, E_____,

   G_____, and C_____.

8. Can you think of two places to which he wrote two letters?

   _____ and _____.

9. Paul was imprisoned in _____, _____, for

   preaching the gospel.

10. In Paul's letters he called himself a _____

127

and an _____ of Jesus Christ.

11. Paul suffered many hardships and persecutions to present Christ. Can you re-member some of them? _____

_____

_____

12. When Paul wrote to an area, how did all the churches then get to read the let-ters? _____

13. Paul not only taught Christ to his people the Jews, but also taught the _____ as God directed him to do.

14. In what city did Paul find worshippers of the Goddess Dianna? _____

15. Paul had a vision that asked him to come preach in _____, a part of Europe.

16. Name some of Paul's close companions and friends. _____, _____, _____, _____

17. Paul warned Christians of _____ who would want to lead them from God's word.

18. Two young men were very close to Paul — in fact, he called them his sons. They were _____ and _____.

19. Paul taught continuously about F_____, L_____, and G_____.

20. Paul's last written letter was _____

21. At the end of his life Paul said He had "_____ a good fight, finished the _____ and kept the _____."

22. Where is this statement found in the New Testament? _____

23. The life of Paul was very interesting if you studied and kept your lessons up. He left so many good examples and teachings for us in these letters. What do you think Paul's reward is from God? _____.

HEBREWS
WRITTEN TO HEBREW CHRISTIANS AROUND JERUSALEM
MEMORY VERSE: Hebrews 2:7

The author is unknown—one comment made is "only God knows" who actually wrote it down originally. Because of persecutions, these Jewish Christians were considering going back to the "old Mosaic way." The writer of this book encourages them to hold fast to their belief of Jesus Christ as their Savior and Lord. The 11th chapter of this writing is sometimes called "The Roll Call of the Heroes of Faith."

1. Chapter 1:1-2 God spoke long ago through the _____ but

   now, in the last days He speaks through His Son,

   _____ who he appointed _____

   to all things and also through whom the _____ was made.

2. Chapter 1:5-14 Jesus is superior to angels, for to which angel did God say "You

   are my _____, today have I _____ you"?

   (vs. 5) AND "You Lord, in the beginning laid the foundation of the

   _____; and the _____ are the works of your

   _____." (vs. 10)

3. Chapter 2:1-3 We must pay closer attention to what we have

   _____, so that we do not _____ away from it, for if

   the _____ spoken through angels proved _____, and

   every _____ received a just penalty, how will we escape if we

   _____ so great a salvation?

4. Chapter 3 (vs. 1) Jesus is H_____ P_____ of our confession

   who was faithful to Him who appointed Him, as was _____. But

   the people led by Moses (vs. 17) angered Him for _____ years and fell in the

   _____.

5. Chapter 5:5-6 So also Christ did not glorify Himself to become a

   _____, but He who said to Him, "You are a

Priest _____ according to the order of Melchizedek. (We will talk about Melchizedek in class).

6. Chapter 9:11-12 But when Christ appeared as a high priest of the _____ to come, He entered through the greater and more _____ tabernacle, not made with _____, and not through the _____ of goats and calves, but through His own _____, having obtained eternal _____.

7. Chapter 10:24-25 Let us consider how to stimulate one _____ to love and _____, not forsaking our own _____ together, as is the _____ of some, but encouraging one _____, and all the more as you see the _____ drawing nigh.

8. Chapter 11 This is the "Faith" chapter talked about and read so often. (vs. 1) Now _____ is the assurance of things _____ for, the conviction of things _____ seen.

This chapter contains so many men of faith from the Old Testament. We will spend some time going over this chapter. While studying for this lesson, please read the whole chapter.

9. Chapter 12:1-2 Let us set aside sin which so easily entangles us, and let us _____ with _____ the race set before us, fixing our eyes on _____, who for the joy set before Him _____ the _____, despising the shame and has sat down at the _____ of God.

10. Chapter 13:15-16 Through Him, let us continually _____ up a sacrifice of praise to God, that is, the _____ of lips that give thanks to His name, and do not _____ doing good and sharing, for with such _____ God is pleased.

WE WILL USE THIS SPACE FOR WRITING DOWN SOME INFO ON CHAPTER 11.

_____

_____

_____

_____

_____

_____

_____

_____

_____

_____

_____

_____

JAMES
CONSIDERED A GENERAL EPISTLE FOR CHRISTIANS
MEMORY VERSE: 1 Corinthians 13:1

The author of this Epistle is James a brother of Jesus. We should not confuse him with James the apostle, or James the son of Alphaeus. This Epistle is written to stress Christian living; not only in truth but in action. True faith is seen in a good life.

CHAPTER 1

1. Vs. 1 — James Identifies himself as a _____ of God and of the Lord _____ Christ This letter was written to the _____

2. Vs. 8 — A _____ man is unstable in all his ways. What does this mean? We will discuss this in class.

3. Vs. 27 explains our duty as a Christian. It is also our privilege, "To visit the _____ and _____ in their affliction, and to keep himself _____ from the world."

CHAPTER 2

4. Read vs. 19-24 to discuss in class. Vs. 23 states that Abraham was a _____ of God. Isn't that wonderful? Are you a friend of God?

CHAPTER 3

5. Vs. 7. Mentions how animals, birds and things of the sea can be tamed, but in vs. 8 it states the _____ can not be tamed.

Read vs. 9-10 for discussion in class. You might want to put some notes down on these two verses.

_____

_____

CHAPTER 4

6. Vs. 7-8. Submit yourselves therefore to _____. _____ the devil and he will flee from you. Draw nigh

132

to _____ and he will draw nigh to _____.

7. Vs. 10. We sing a song in our worship with these words,

    "_____ yourselves in the sight of the _____

    and He will _____ you up."

8. We make plans and say we are going to do thus and so. In vs. 15, we find

    that we should add this statement to our plans. "_____ the Lord _____,"

    we shall do thus and so.

CHAPTER 5

9. Vs 12. But above all things, my brethren, _____,

    neither by Heaven, neither by the _____, neither by any

    other _____: but let your _____ be _____, and

    your _____, _____, lest ye fall into condemnation. So do

    you think from this scripture you could lose your soul over evil talk?

10. Vs. 14. If there are any sick among you, let him call for the

    _____ of the _____ and let them

    _____ over him, _____ him with _____

    in the name of the Lord.

11. Vs. 16. Christians are told to pray for one another. It is always so comfort-

    ing when someone cares and prays for you whether for sickness or for

    other troubles that may come into your life.

The effectual _____ prayer of a righteous

_____ availeth much.

1 PETER

THIS LETTER WAS WRITTEN AND PASSED AROUND FROM AREA TO AREA

MEMORY VERSE: 1 Peter 5:8

Peter wrote to Jew and Gentile Christians. Peter was an apostle. His name was changed from Simon to Peter by the Lord. Peter's name means "a rock" or "stone." Peter was with Jesus, he saw all Jesus did, he heard what Jesus said. Peter writes to encourage Christians to live like Christ.

CHAPTER 1

1. Vs. 1, He states he is an _____ of Jesus Christ

2. Vs. 2, He addresses God the Father, God the Spirit, and God the Christ. We can't really understand this, but we know they are one; and through Christ's blood we have_____ and _____.

3. Vs. 14-15 As _____ children, be _____ as he which called you is _____; so be ye _____ in all manner of _____.

4. Vs. 19 We are redeemed by the _____ blood of Christ as a lamb without _____ or _____.

5. Vs. 22 See that you _____ one another with a pure heart _____.

6. Vs. 23 Being _____ again, by the _____ of God and which _____ and _____ forever.

CHAPTER 2

7. Vs. 9 But _____ are a chosen _____, a _____ priesthood, an _____ nation, a _____ people; that ye should shew forth the praises of Him who has _____ you out of _____ in-to His _____ light.

8. Vs 13-14, _____ yourselves to every ordinance of man for

134

the _____ sake whether it be for Kings or Governors. (In other words, obey the laws).

9. Vs. 17, Honor the _____. _____ the brother-hood

CHAPTER 3

10. Vs. 1, _____ be in subjection to your own husband. What does subjection mean?

_____

_____

11. Vs. 7, Husbands give _____ unto your _____ as being _____ together of the _____ of life.

12. Vs. 15, Be ready always to _____ an answer to every man that _____ a reason of the _____ that is within you.

CHAPTER 4

13. Vs. 11, If any man _____ let him speak as the _____ of God.

14. Vs. 15-16, But let none of you suffer as a _____ or a _____, or as an _____, or as a _____. But, if you suffer as a _____ do not be _____, but let him _____ God.

CHAPTER 5

15. Vs 6-7, Humble yourselves therefore under the _____ hand of God that he may exalt you in due _____; _____ all your cares on _____ for he _____ for you.

16. Vs. 11, To him be glory and _____ forever and forever. Amen.

2 PETER

THIS SECOND LETTER IS ADDRESSED TO
THE SAME PERSONS AS THE FIRST

MEMORY VERSE: Acts 9:34

In this writing there is concern over the false teachers and evildoers who have come into the church. Teaching on how to deal with this situation is included as well as the subject of Jesus' return.

Chapter 1

In this chapter after identifying himself as a servant and apostle, Peter points

out some traits for Christian living: Applying all _____, in

your faith, supply _____ and in your moral excellence,

knowledge, and in your knowledge _____, and in your

self-control, perseverance, and in your _____, godliness,

and in your godliness, brotherly kindness, and in your

_____, love. (vs. 5-7).

Chapter 2:20-21

For if, after they have escaped the defilements of the _____ by the

knowledge of the Lord and Savior Jesus Christ, they are again

_____ in them and overcome, the last state is _____

than the first. For it would be _____ for them not to have known the

_____ of righteousness, than having known it, to turn away from the

holy _____ handed on to them. (vs. 22) Like a dog returns to

its own _____, and a _____, after washing, returns to

_____ in the mire.

Chapter 3:10

But the _____ of the Lord will come like a _____, in

which the _____ will pass away with a roar, and the

_____ will be destroyed with intense _____,

and the _____ and it's works will be _____ up.
(vs. 18) Grow in the _____ and knowledge of our Lord and
Savior, _____. To Him be the _____, both
now and to the _____ of eternity. Amen.

1 JOHN
A PASS AROUND LETTER

MEMORY VERSE: I John 5:13

John, an apostle, a fisherman, the son of Zebedee. He was concerned about false teachers coming in to cause confusion. He states that God is light and in Him is no darkness.

CHAPTER 1

Vs. 1-2 John writes about the "Word of Life" and says He is what we (apostles) have _____, what we have _____ with our eyes, what we have looked at and _____ with our hands. The "Word" (Christ) we have seen and proclaim to you, eternal life which was with the Father. We proclaim to you also that you too might have _____ with us and our _____ is with the _____ and the Son Jesus Christ.

Vs. 5 states that God is light and in Him is no _____.

In vs. 7, if we walk in the light as He is in the _____, we have _____ with one another and the _____ of Jesus cleanses us from all _____.

CHAPTER 2

John writes to commend them on their belief. He writes in vs. 12-14, to _____ children, to fathers, young _____, children. The word of God abides in them and they have overcome the

_____.

CHAPTER 3

Vs. 1, See how great a _____ the Father has bestowed on us, that we would be called _____ of God, and such we are.

Vs. 16, we know _____ by this, that He laid down His _____ for us and we ought to lay down our _____ for the _____.

138

Vs. 21-22. Beloved, if our _____ does not condemn us, we have _____ before God and whatever we ask we receive from _____. Because we keep his commandments and do the _____ that are pleasing in His sight.

CHAPTER 4

Vs. 7, _____, let us love _____, for love is from _____, and everyone who loves is _____ of God, and knows _____.

Vs. 20 — If someone says, "I _____ God," and _____ his brother, he is a liar, for the _____ who does not love his _____, whom he has seen, cannot love _____ whom he has not seen.

CHAPTER 5

Vs. 3 For this is the _____ of God, that we keep his _____, and his commandments are not _____

Vs. 13 These are the things I have _____ to you who _____ in the name of the _____ of _____, so that you know you have _____.

Vs. 21 — Little _____, guard yourselves from _____.

2 JOHN
LOVE MAKES US OBEDIENT
MEMORY VERSE: John 3:16

Vs.3 Grace, mercy and _____ will be with us, from God the

_____ and from _____ the Son of the

_____, in truth and love.

Vs. 7 For many _____ have gone out into the

_____, those who do not _____ Jesus Christ has

come in the _____. This is the deceiver and the

_____.

Vs. 12 Though I have many things to _____ to you, I do not want to

do so with _____ and _____; but I hope to come to you and speak

_____ to _____, so that your _____ may be made full.

3 JOHN
WALK IN THE TRUTH
MEMORY VERSE: I John 5:2

One Chapter To This Letter. Read the whole chapter.

The beloved apostle John wrote these 3 books, plus the Gospel of John and also Revelation.

He writes this letter to a friend, _____. He _____

that Gaius has good _____ and that his _____ prospers. He

knows that he is _____ in the _____. Gaius is a beloved friend.

John thinks men who spread the word should have some support from the brethren. But, when he wrote something to the _____, D_____

did not accept what he said, so when he comes he will set things straight.

He also mentions Demetrius, who has received _____ from everyone.

THE ONE WHO DOES GOOD IS OF GOD; THE ONE WHO DOES EVIL

HAS NOT SEEN GOD. (Found in vs. _____)

JUDE
A GENERAL EPISTLE,
WARNING AGAINST FALSE TEACHINGS

MEMORY VERSE: Name the 12 Apostles

Jude identifies himself as a brother of James and it is assumed he is also a brother to Jesus. Jesus' brothers all became preachers (1 Corinthians 9:5). Jude is concerned about false teachers, ones teaching something besides what the apostles and Jesus taught. We must guard the truth carefully. Jude's epistle is written for all Christians of that day, as well as for our learning today.

1. Vs. 3. Ye should _____ contend for the _____

   which was once delivered to the _____.

2. Vs. 4. This verse talks about ungodly men who would turn the

   _____ God has given us into sinful acts denying the Lord

   _____ and his teachings.

3. Vs. 6. Even angels who kept not their place, he hath reserved

   _____ and _____ until the judgment.

4. Vs. 7. Remember the fate of two towns which were so evil that God de-

   stroyed them (in Abraham's time)? They are the cities of

   _____ and _____.

5. Vs. 17-19. But remember the words spoken by the apostles of our Lord

   _____ how they told you there would be

   _____ who walk ungodly and have not the _____.

6. Vs. 21. Keep yourselves in the _____ of _____, looking

   for the mercy of our Lord Jesus Christ unto

   _____.

7. Vs. 25. To our wise _____ our _____ be

   _____and majesty, _____ and

   _____ forever. Amen.

Prophecy

REVELATION
AN ACCOUNT OF PROPHECIES

MEMORY VERSE: Genesis 2:29

Revelation has _____ chapters.

Revelation was written by _____the apostle, who also wrote the gospel of _____and 1, 2, and 3 _____.

1. In Revelation 1:4, John writes to the 7 _____ of

    _____. _____ and _____ be unto you from

    Him (Jesus) _____ is, and _____ was, and _____ is to

    come.

2. Warnings were given to these churches about things they were doing that were not true to their previous teachings. As instructions were given to each of these churches, a statement is made. Look at 2:7, 11, 17; 29, 3:6, 13, 22. Write the statement.

    _____

    _____

3. List the 7 churches in chapter 2 and 3 that received the warning.

    a. (2:1) _____

    b. (2:8) _____

    c. (2:12) _____

    d. (2:18) _____

    e. (3:1) _____

    f. (3:7) _____

    g. (3:14) _____

4. To which church was this statement made? "Thy works are neither cold or hot, so because you are lukewarm, I will spew you out of my mouth"?

    _____

5. Chapter 1:7 indicates, as we have studied before, about Jesus coming again, that he will come in the _____ and every _____ shall see Him.

6. Jesus said, "I am the _____ and the _____," which indicates the _____ and the _____. (1:11)

7. Chapter 22:18-19. In these verses are warnings concerning teachings and prophesies of this book. "If any man shall _____ unto these things, God shall add _____ that are written in this book and if any man shall_____ from the words of the book of this prophecy, God shall take away his _____ out of the book of life. Let's discuss this further in class, be ready.

As the book of Genesis gives the creation story and, at the beginning, the first promise of the Savior, so Revelation at the close of the Bible sets forth the glory and majesty of Christ in His second coming. He came first in humiliation but will come the second time in exaltation.

THE END

WHAT MUST I DO TO BE SAVED?

ACTS 16:30

That question was asked by the jailer in Philippi when Paul and Silas were imprisoned for teaching about Jesus. The same question has been asked over and over down through time when man realized he cannot save himself. Perhaps you have thought about this question too, since all of us want to go to heaven. Well, guess what! The answer given by Paul and Silas to the Philippian jailer so many years ago is still a good answer today. REMEMBER God's word never changes, Jesus never changes—Hebrews 13:8.

Some of you might already be Christians and some of you may be giving thought to becoming a Christian. Let's take a look at the answer Paul and Silas gave the jailer in Acts 16:31-33. (Read this scripture).

In Acts 2, when the church had it's beginning and Peter preached the first sermon about Jesus being the savior, the people who were there asked the same question. Read Acts 2:37 and write the question.

_____

_____

Romans 10:17 States we must _____ God's word in order to have faith.

Hebrews 11:6 He who comes to God must _____ that He is.

Acts 17:30 God commands all men to _____ .

Matthew 10:32 Jesus said whoever would _____ me before men, He would confess in Heaven.

Acts 2:38 Peter told those present to be _____ for remission of their sins.

Jesus' Kingdom is the Church. To be a member of Christ's Church we must obey all the steps listed above, and in Acts 2:41 and 47 we read that God adds us to the Church. We do not join the Church.

There are other scriptures that support the statements of obedience above. But, how many times must God tell us something for us to know He means what he says?

After our sins are washed away, or remitted (forgiven) as in Acts 2:38, we continue to study and grow in God's word. We learn by reading our Bible, attending

146

Bible classes and worship. Worship is a commandment to Christians by example of the early Church who met on the first day of the week to sing, pray, study, give and take the Lord's supper in memory of Jesus' death. In Hebrews 10:25 we are told "_____ to forsake the assembling of ourselves together."

As Christians we make a promise to God. In deciding to become a Christian we must consider the responsibility that goes with being a Christian. We know we can never be perfect as Christ was perfect but we can strive to do our best.

Along the way in your life, you will hear someone say another way is as good as God's way—if you are only sincere. For your memory work read Matthew 7:21. Read it through twice. Does it sound like God will accept those who do not obey his will? We will discuss this in our class time.

The Keys of Salvation

1.

2. HEAR

So faith comes from hearing and hearing by the word of Christ. Rom. 10:17

3. BELIEVE

And without faith it is impossible to please Him, for He who comes to God must believe that He is, and that He is a rewarder of those who seek Him. Heb 11:6

4. REPENT

Therefor having overlooked the times of ignorance, God is now declaring to men that all everywhere should repent. Acts 17:30

5. CONFESS

"for with the heart man believes resulting in righteousness and with the mouth he confesses, resulting in salvation" Rom. 10:10

6. BE BAPTIZED

Repent and let each of you be baptized in the name of Jesus Christ for the forgiveness of your sins and you shall receive the gift of the Holy Spirit. Acts 2:38

7. BE FAITHFUL

Be faithful unto death, and I will give you the crown of Life. Rev. 2:10

148

www.ingramcontent.com/pod-product-compliance
Lightning Source LLC
Chambersburg PA
CBHW080958120626
46546CB00010B/2948